Marine Fighting Squadron One-Twenty-One (VMF-121)

By Tom Doll

Color By Don Greer

squadron/signal publications

Captain Joe Foss shot down five Zero fighters on 25 October 1942, while his Commanding Officer, Major "Duke" Davis added to the squadron's score with a Zero and a Betty of his own, making him an ace.

If you have any photographs of aircraft, armor, soldiers or ships of any nation, particularly wartime snapshots, why not share them with us and help make Squadron/Signal's books all the more interesting and complete in the future. Any photograph sent to us will be copied and the original returned. The donor will be fully credited for any photos used. Please send them to:

Squadron/Signal Publications, Inc.
1115 Crowley Drive.
Carrollton, TX 75011-501010

Если у вас есть фотографии самолётов, вооружения кораблей любой страны, особенно, снимки времён і поделитесь с нами и помогите сделать новые книг Эскадрон/Сигнал ещё интереснее. Мы переснимем фотографии и вернём оригиналы. Имена приславш будут сопровождать все опубликованные фотограф Пожалуйста, присылайте фотографии по адресу:

Squadron/Signal Publications, Inc.
1115 Crowley Drive.
Carrollton, TX 75011-501010

軍用機、装甲車両、兵士、軍艦などの写真を所持しておられる方はいらっしゃいませんか？どの国ものでも結構です。作戦中に撮影されたものが特に良いのです。Squadron/Signal社の出版する刊行において、このような写真は内容を一層充実し、興味深くすることができます。当方にお送り頂い写真は、複写の後お返しいたします。出版物中に写真を使用した場合は、必ず提供者のお名前を明させて頂きます。お写真は下記にご送付ください。

Acknowledgements

Before an author can even begin to put pen to paper in a project such as this book, he must enlist the assistance of a great many people. The following individuals exhibited extreme cooperation and courtesy, not to mention long suffering.

Thank you very much for helping make the VMF-121 story as complete as possible. There are many facets to the history of VMF-121 and the author has covered as many as possible within the format.
Semper Fi.

Elmo Allen	Tony Betchik
Sandia Bethel	A.J. Bibee
Steve Blake, "Fighter Pilots in Aerial Combat"	
COL J. Ward Boyce, USAF, Ret.	George Burianic
Lieutenant Colonel L. Tolar Bryan, USMC, Ret.	
Perry N. Coley	Robert J. Cressman
LTCOL Philip L. Crawford, USMC, Ret.	Harry Gann
MSGT Walter F. "Fritz" Gemeinhardt, USMC, Ret.	
Guadalcanal Echoes Quarterly	Ardy Jahan, Printec
Berkley R. Jackson	Clay Jansson
Charles Kilborn	Robert L.Lawson
COLHamilton Lawrence, USMC, Ret.	Audrey Mann
CAPT Richard M. Loughery, USMC, Ret.	Frank J. Mayer
Marine Corps Aviation Association	William A. Riley
LTCOL Thomas H. Mann, Jr., USMC, Ret.	
GYSGT Leroy M. McCallum, USMC, Ret.	Walter J. Meyer
National Archives and Records Center	John Rohrbach
COL R. Bruce Porter, USMC, Ret.	Jim Sullivan
John E. Schuler	Perry L. Shuman
Roger Seybel, Grumman History Center	David Steinbacher
Wilber H. "Bud" Stuckey	USAAC
USAAF	USMC
William J. VerMeulen	USN
COL Kenneth Walsh, USMC, Ret.	

Dedications

This work could very well be Tony Betchik's book. Tony put most of his adult life into compiling information about VMF-121. He spent most of 1942 with the squadron and earned his stripes on Guadalcanal. Tony's hard work and long hours assured that VMF-121's story would not fade from history. He made it all possible.

George Burianic has devoted a large part of his life to preserving the history of VMF-121. He keeps the squadron alive and made it possible for the author to contact many of 121's former members. George was with the Peleliu group and his active participation in squadron activities is well known.

This book is respectfully dedicated to Tony Betchik and George Burianic. Their kind assistance and courteous demeanor never wavered.

Overleaf: A F4F-4 of VMF-121 parked in a revetment at Kearney Mesa during July of 1942. There is a line running from the wheel chock to the pitot tube cover. This was done as a precaution against leaving the pitot cover on which could cause a great deal of trouble for the pilot. (Perry N. Coley via R.L. Lawson)

INTRODUCTION

This book was made possible through the hard work and dedication of the men who lived it. They put their lives on the line pursuing an inherently dangerous profession made even more hazardous by the Japanese attack on Pearl Harbor of 7 December 1941. Although this work concerns the Second World War activities of Marine Fighting Squadron One-Twenty-One, it could be the story of any Second World War Marine Corps fighter squadron.

Naval aviators are unique and although designated as Naval Aviators, Marine Aviators are a breed apart. The same can be said about the dedicated men that kept their F4F Wildcats and F4U Corsairs in the air and brought them home again.

Together, the pilots, mechanics, armorers, metalsmiths and other support personnel, endured the misery of Guadalcanal. Through the rain, mud, Japanese and malaria, they emerged the victor. The horrific shelling of 13-14 October 1942, might have discouraged lesser men, but these men endured and prevailed.

As the war moved on into other areas with other strange sounding names, VMF-121 moved along with it. The long, sweaty flights up the Solomon Islands chain and the names New Georgia, Kolombangara, Rendova, Kahili and Bougainville became familiar signposts. Day in and day out, the men of VMF-121 flew their missions, added up the hours and dreamed of home. In time, they too would serve out their tours and just as they had done, others would come and take their place so they could rotate home to their well-earned rest and relaxation.

New personnel began forming around a few of the veteran VMF-121 pilots and support troops at a little spot in the California desert called Mojave. From here came yet another VMF-121. Their war would be just as dangerous but the threat of aerial dogfights and flying against vast flights of Japanese bombers would not be their lot. Fourth tour VMF-121 pilots flew the most dangerous of all missions; close air support. Low-level strafing and bombing in support of Marines on the ground brought the pilots right down on the deck. If hit in a vital spot at that altitude, recovery could be very difficult, if not impossible. From Peleliu, VMF-121 performed the job given them and in the end helped to bring about the demise of the Japanese Empire and its ambitious leaders.

VMF-121 was the fifth Marine Corps fighting squadron to enter combat with the enemy during the Second World War. They were preceded by VMF-211 at Wake Island, VMF-221 at Midway, and VMF-223 and VMF-224 on Guadalcanal.

VMF-121 was already in existence at the beginning of the war and they witnessed the final victory. They amassed a total of enemy aircraft shot down that was second to none. One of their pilots, Captain Joe Foss, earned the Medal of Honor while with VMF-121. Another, former VMF-121 pilot, Lieutenant Ken Walsh, earned the Medal of Honor while flying with VMF-124.

The support crews assigned to VMF-121 were among the best in the Marine Corps. Many were sighted for their outstanding and courageous work, often under fire and always under the most primitive working conditions

At the time of this writing, the men of VMF-121's Second World War era, are in their "Golden Years." At each squadron reunion the ranks are diminished by one or two and the ravages of time keeps a few more from attending. The memories and spirit of their youth are still present and, while they would not trade their experiences with VMF-121 for anything, they would not like to do it over again.

We, who enjoyed the comfort and security of the United States during that terrible war, owe it, in no small way, to the men of VMF-121 and to all those who gave their all.

1941

In July of 1938, the authorized strength of United States Naval Aviation was 3,000 aircraft. The Navy Department sought and Congress granted an increase to 10,000 aircraft during June of 1940. The following month, this was raised to 15,000 aircraft. The "two-ocean" Navy was well on it's way.

Marine Corps Aviation immediately prior to our entry into the Second World War, had benefited from the Naval Expansion Act of 17 May 1938. During the first half of 1940, Marine Corps aviation strength reached a peak of 139 aircraft, operated by 200 commissioned officers, nineteen warrant officers and 1,324 enlisted men.

During those immediate pre-war years Marine Corps aviation was composed of nine operating squadrons. Four were stationed at San Diego, California; four at Turner Field, Quantico, Virginia and one at Bourne Field, Saint Thomas, Virgin Islands. All were attached to the Fleet Marine Force with a senior aviator on the staff of the Commanding General of that Force to coordinate their training.

The four squadrons at Quantico were known as the First Marine Aircraft Group and were composed of one fighting, one scouting, one bombing and one utility squadron. These units trained with the First Brigade of the Fleet Marine Force and participated in annual maneuvers with that organization.

The same type of squadrons made up the Second Marine Aircraft Group at San Diego, California. They worked with the Second Brigade

The newly formed VMF-121 flew Grumman F3F-2 fighters on loan from VMF-1 based at Quantico, Virginia. Many of the pilots assigned to the new squadron also came from VMF-1. In July of 1941, VMF-121 began taking delivery of their new Grumman F4F-3 fighters. By that time, VMF-1 had been redesignated VMF-111 and it too began transitioning to the new fighter from Grumman. (USMC)

Grumman F3F-2s of VMF-1 on the ramp at Saint Thomas, Virgin Islands, during manuevers held in 1939. Some of these would be loaned to VMF-121 for training. (LeRoy McCallum)

of the Fleet Marine Force. They were also attached to the Aircraft Battle Force for fleet operations which included carrier training. Most of their flying was carried out with the Fleet.

In Saint Thomas, the squadron was known as VMS-3 (Marine Scouting Squadron - Three). Immediately prior to the Second World War, this squadron operated Grumman J2F-2As.

Marine Corps Reserve Aviation was also well represented during the pre-war years. Marine Aviation Reservists totaled 100 officers and 600 enlisted men. They participated in forty-eight drills and two weeks of active duty annually. In addition, there were about thirty officers and 300 enlisted men in the Volunteer Reserve, who, though unable to attend regular drills, were available and partially trained to help fill the gap should a need arise.

The Reserve supported ten squadrons on ten Naval Reserve Air Bases throughout the United States. These were:

VMS-lR	Sguantum (Boston) Massachusetts
VMS-2R	Brooklyn, New York
VMS-3R	Anacostia, D.C.
VMS-4R	Miami (Opa Locka) Florida
VMS-5R	Gross Isle (Detroit) Michigan
VMS-6R	Minneapolis, Minnesota
VMS-7R	Long Beach, California
VMS-8R	Oakland, California
VMS-9R	Seattle, Washington
VMS-10R	Kansas City, Missouri

1941 saw the birth of four new squadrons within Marine Corps Aviation. These were: VMF-121 (24 June 1941), VMO-1 (24 June 1941), VMF-221 (11 July 1941), and VM0-251 (1 December 1941. That same year, on 1 July, Marine squadrons were redesignated. Those redesignated were:

Quantico
VMF-1 to VMF-111
VMS-1 to VMSB-131
VMB-1 to VMSB-132
VMJ-1 to VMJ-152
VMO-1 to VMO-151

San Diego
VMF-2 to VMF-211
VMS-2 to VMSB-231
VMB-2 to VMSB-232
VMJ-2 to VMJ-252

St. Thomas
VMS-3 remained VMS-3

The Marine Corps continued it's expansion as 1941 moved along

Pilots VMF-121 at New Berne, North Carolina in September of 1941. (Tech Sergeant Joseph J. Palko, 1st Lieutenant Robert Fraser and 2nd Lieutenant R. Bruce Porter have no photographs available)

Major Sam Jack was the first commanding officer of VMF-121. He took command on 24 June 1941 at Quantico, Virginia. (L. Tolar Bryan)

Captain John P. Condon was the squadron's Executive Officer. (L. Tolar Bryan)

Captain Elmer E. Brackett, Jr. Division Leader. (L. Tolar Bryan)

1st Lieutenant Richard M. "Jake" Baker. (L. Tolar Bryan)

1st Lieutenant William A. Rygg. (L. Tolar Bryan)

1st Lieutenant Paul H. Ashley. (L. Tolar Bryan)

2nd Lieutenant Hamilton Lawrence. (L. Tolar Bryan)

2nd Lieutenant Cecil B "Blackie" Brewer. (L. Tolar Bryan)

2nd Lieutenant Philip L. Crawford. (L. Tolar Bryan)

2nd Lieutenant L. Tolar Bryan. (L. Tolar Bryan)

2nd Lieutenant Wallace H. Cloake. (L. Tolar Bryan)

2nd Lieutenant Joseph F. Quilty, Jr. (L. Tolar Bryan)

2nd Lieutenant Edwin C. Fry (L. Tolar Bryan)

Technical Sergeant Alexander Thomson, NAP. (L. Tolar Bryan)

2nd Lieutenant Kenneth R. Chamberlain. (L. Tolar Bryan)

Technical Sergeant Pharron C. Cooke, NAP. (L. Tolar Bryan)

Technical Sergeant Kenneth A. Walsh, NAP. (L. Tolar Bryan)

Lieutenant (JG) "Doc" Hinman, USN (MC) VMF-121's Flight Surgeon. (L. Tolar Bryan)

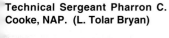

toward that fateful December. On 1 February, the First and Second Brigades of the Fleet Marine Force were officially activated as the First and Second Marine Divisions, respectively. New enlistees would soon begin filling the ranks of these new organizations.

On 28 May, a company of parachutists was formed at Quantico. Marine parachutists had been training on the parachute tower at Lakehurst, New Jersey, since the previous October. As the troops became qualified in the new technique, usually within two weeks, they transferred to Quantico for additional training and conditioning. This was followed by actual jump training from an aircraft. By August, the First Parachute Battalion had been formed.

Marine Fighting Squadron One-Twenty-One had it's formal beginning on Tuesday, 24 June 1941 at Quantico, Virginia. All the squadrons of MAG-1 were assembled outside the main hangars with the new squadron in the center. The ranking officer present was Major General Holland M. Smith. Also present , among others, was Lieutenant Colonel Louis E. Woods. VMF-121's Commanding Officer was Major Samuel Sloan Jack. He had been born 9 August 1905, had been appointed from Arizona to the U. S. Naval Academy, graduating in 1927. Jack, a veteran of the Marine Corps Nicaraguan campaign, accepted and read the orders giving him command of the new squadron.

He was then congratulated by General Smith. Major Jack then thanked the assembled group and left the platform as all hands marched off with a feeling of pride in their new squadron.

At the time of commissioning, VMF-121 had been training with three Grumman F3F-2s borrowed from VMF-1. Their own Grumman F4F-3s were not scheduled for delivery until July. These F4Fs would be among a number of new Grummans (BuNos 3970-4057) that were delivered to VMF-221, VMF-211, VMF-121, as well as VF-3 and VF-5 during the period July to September of 1941. Most of these later saw combat.

By the time the squadron started taking delivery of their new aircraft the First Marine Aircraft Wing had come into existance, under the command of Lieutenant Colonel Woods. The new wing was composed of a Headquarters Squadron and Marine Air Group-1. This occurred at the same time that all Marine. squadrons were redesignated on 1 July.

VMF-121 was rapidly getting its training cycle underway. By 29 August, the unit had begun operating out of a grassy field located at New Bern, North Carolina. They flew their new F4F-3s on a daily basis, practicing air-to-air gunnery and conducting field carrier landing practice (FCLP). Being only one of two F4F squadrons in the Marine Corps, VMF-111 being the other, VMF-121 was tasked with working out new tactics using the F4F.

Typical of the new pilots coming into the squadron was 2nd Lieutenant Philip L. Crawford. He reported to VMF-121 on 19 August 1941. Like many, he had not flown the F4F and was looking forward to the experience. Familiarization flights were the order of the day within the squadron at the time. Section tactics and IBP (Individual Battle Practice) using the gun camera, also figured in his routine. At the time, night flying was something that would be accomplished in the future.

Crawford would soon have his first taste of F4F-3 night flying, unscheduled. From time to time when the aircraft needed major work, they would be flown up to Quantico. When they were ready to be returned someone from the squadron would fly up and pick them up. This also applied to picking up new fighters as they became available.

Around noon on 7 October, the Operations Officer informed Crawford and TSGT Pharron C. Cooke, that they were to proceed to Quantico in the squadron's SNJ-3 to pick up two F4Fs that were ready to be returned to the squadron at New Bern. They flew the SNJ up to Quantico and got the F4Fs ready for the return flight to New Bern. By then it was getting a little late but Crawford figured they could make it back before dark. It was an hour before sunset and he knew the little fighter could make the trip in just about an hour, which left no time to spare. He had made the flight before and was sure he could make it back before dark.

At a point about twenty minutes out of New Bern, Crawford started

Factory-fresh F4F-3 fighters parked on the grass at the Grumman facility ready for delivery to VMF-121. At this time, the Wildcats were painted overall Light Gray with White squadron codes and small national insignia. (Grumman)

getting a little concerned about available daylight. The sun was going down and it was starting to get dark. The ground beneath the two pilots was not too familiar and he recalled that about five minutes beyond the field was the ocean.

In the meantime, VMF-121's Executive Officer, Captain John Condon, had received the flight advisory that the two pilots had left Quantico and would be arriving at New Bern at sundown without having any night flying time in the F4F. On top of everything else, the dirt strip at the squadron's location had no lights. Crawford felt that Condon was probably ready to scratch two planes and their pilots.

Condon had flare pots set out along the strip and lined-up cars along the first part of the strip so they could shine their lights on the part of the runway where they were supposed to land. They then started listening for the two Wildcats, so they could light the pots and turn on the car lights.

Meanwhile, Crawford was cruising nervously along, hoping his compass had been swung at Quantico. Cooke was hanging trustingly right on his wing. Fortunately, right on time and right in front of them, the lights started showing up. What a relief for Crawford. He still had to land, however, and, as they broke for their landings, it was now starting to get really dark. Fortunately, both pilots made smooth and uneventful landings. Crawford and his wingman were now safely on the ground and as he began to feel good about his ability, Condon got a hold of him and cast considerable doubt on his good judgment. The XO did, howev-

er, grudgingly, comment that he thought they did a good job of bringing the Wildcats into the field.

During the squadron's stay at New Bern, part of their training with the F4F involved towing target sleeves. It was not considered a successful takeoff with the target sleeve if the pilot let the sleeve drag the ground while taking off. The mechanics and ordanancemen would criticize the enlisted pilots if this happened. Taking off with the sleeve could be very dangerous. TSGT Alexander Thomson received quite a lecture from Major Leonard K. Davis when it appeared that he almost stalled out his F4F on a sleeve take off when the squadron was stationed at Kearney Mesa. Alex's sleeve never touched the ground, but the F4F almos

A line-up of Grumman F4F-3s of VMF-121 on the flight line at New Bern, North Carolina during September of 1941. The aircraft in the foreground is 121-F-15. The White squadron codes were sometimes difficult to see against the Light Gray camouflage. (R. Bruce Porter)

The full complement of F4F Wildcats on the flight line at New Bern, North Carolina, during September of 1941. 121-F-2 heads the line and has wheel chocks and tie downs attached to the wing and tail. (Phil Crawford)

stalled before Alex leveled off at the tip of a steep climb.

Towing targets was not the safest duty. Case in point was VMF-121's TSGT Leroy M. McCallum. Just before VMF-1 experienced their reorganization, Leroy McCallum made a tow target run in a Grumman J2F-4. The minimum length for towing a sleeve was 900 feet, but McCallum normally ran his line at 1,500 feet as an extra measure of safety. The J2F pilot was 2nd Lieutenant R. M. Nelson. 2nd Lieutenant E. B.

Major Jack and Captain Brackett enjoy a light moment during flight operations at New Bern. The training schedule for the new squadron was hectic and intense, including air-to-air gunnery, navigation and indoctrination flights in their new fighters. (R. Bruce Porter)

The Grumman F4F-3 was the best fighter available to the Marines during 1941 and they were rapidly re-equipping all first line fighter squadrons. (R. Bruce Porter)

Pennington, Jr. made his run on the sleeve, misjudged his aim and hit the J2F. McCallum felt his foot go numb and looked down expecting to see a bloody foot. Luckily, what he saw was a missing heel on his shoe. He then observed a hole in the fuselage fuel tank and managed to plug the leak as best he could with a lead pencil. In the event, the J2F, Nelson and McCallum all made it safely back to Guantanamo, Cuba.

New Bern Field was actually part of the Simmons-Nott Airport, named in honor of North Carolina Senator F.M. Simmons and 2nd Lieutenant Joel D. Nott, USMC. The airport was originally slated to be named in honor of Senator Simmons, however, due to a tragic event that took place on 21 November 1931, another name was added to the airport's formal name.

During the weekend of the airport's dedication, Marine Fighting Squadron 9 was slated to perform aerial maneuvers for the assembled crowd of dignitaries and townspeople. It was during one of these maneuvers that tragedy occurred. Lieutenant Nott's fighter, a Curtiss F7C-1 (BuNo 7658), was in the process of performing a Lufberry circle along with others of the squadron. The object was to lose altitude gradually and, at the same time, tighten the circle. When low enough, Lieutenant Nott was to break out of the circle into a dive, with each aircraft following to form a line; then, with throttles wide open, dive past the grandstand at about fifty feet off the ground. As the six planes in the circle got lower and the circle tightened, Nott's Curtiss suddenly flipped over into a spin and he crashed to his death.

Senator Simmons, who was present and witnessed the crash, directed that Lieutenant Nott's name be added to the name of the airport in honor of his service to the Marine Corps and to his country.

The squadron carried a number of enlisted pilots on its roster during the early months and took a few of these pre-war NAP's (Naval Aviation Pilots) with them to Guadalcanal in 1942. One such NAP was Technical Sergeant Joseph J. Palko. Palko was liked by all and had a wonderful sense of humor. At about the same time that VMF-121 was forming at Quantico, the American Volunteer Group (AVG) was gathering pilots from the U.S. services to fly for China in their war against the Japanese. Three pilots from VMF-1, 2nd Lieutenants Thomas C. Haywood, Kenneth Jernstedt and Charles H. Older, joined the new group. When the three former-Marine pilots came through the squadron's barracks at Quantico to say good-by to the enlisted troops, Joe Palko took special notice.

Shortly after the departure of Haywood, Jernsteadt and Older, Joe Palko came through the barracks making a pitch for volunteers to go to Burma to support the AVG by maintaining their P-40s. Several VMF-121 mechanics, including Master Tech Sergeant Wilbur H. "Bud" Stuckey, signed on. Palko had them convinced that, in view of the historical events taking place in the world, it was the right time for this to happen. It was, of course, one of Palko's many practical jokes. From then on, the group of mechanics that signed on with Palko became known as his "Burma Detail."

The squadron used much of their time at New Bern to learn all they

Phil Crawford and Eddie Fry in the latest 1941 Marine Corps flight gear at the squadron camp at New Bern. Fry later served on Guadalcanal with VMF-121 during their first combat tour. (R. Bruce Porter)

could about their new aircraft and the familiarization flights seemed endless. While at New Bern, VMF-121 witnessed many training jumps of the new Marine Corps Parachute Battalion. Utility Squadron One-Fifty-Two (VMJ-152) provided the Douglas R3D-2 high-winged transports, and near-by Camp Lejeune provided the Marines. On more than one occasion the Paramarines landed just a feet from the squadron's flight line.

In November, the squadron was ordered to Southern Pines, North Carolina, to participate in the U.S. Army's General Headquarters' Carolina maneuvers. Southern Pines is located 130 miles west of New Bern and was approximately two miles west of the western most boundary of Fort Bragg. The men of VMF-121 were to fly in support of Lieutenant General Hugh A. Drum's Blue Army.

Even though they supported the Blue Army, the squadron painters applied large White crosses to both sides of the squadron's Wildcats and to the top and bottom of the wings. Participating U.S. Army aircraft also used this White marking for identification. The opposing Army used a Red cross on their aircraft.

The squadron was part of First Army's First Air Support Command, commanded by Colonel William E. Kepner, U.S. Army. This also included the 3rd Bomber Group and the 6th Pursuit Wing. VMF-121 was temporarily assigned to the 6th PW and operated with this group during the first phase of the maneuvers when they participated in the Battle of the Pee Dee River.

Major Sam Jack led his squadron on many interesting missions in sup-

port of the Blue Army. Lieutenant Colonel L. Tolar Bryan, USMC, Ret., remembers the attacks they made on the bridges across the river. *I remember our dive-bombing the pontoon bridges across the Pee Dee River. We started our dive at about 20,000 feet and dropped our bombs (flour bags) at about 500 feet. Quite a mission.*

Lieutenant Colonel Bryan recalled another squadron mission; *We were involved in a strafing mission against the Red Army at Polk Field located on Fort Bragg. We approached the field at a very low altitude, approximately 100 feet, only to find we were attacking the field at the same time as the Army's parachutists from Fort Bragg were jumping from an altitude that was much higher than we were flying. It was quite a sight to look up and see several parachutists descending toward you from above.*

Phase Two of the Carolina maneuvers found VMF-121 still flying with General Drum's Blue Army, but this time around the Army's 17th Bomber Group joined them as part of the First Air Support Command.

The second Carolina maneuver began at 0630 on 25 November 1941. It was cold and clear and the action was to be known as the Battle of Camden. Camden was little town in South Carolina which was the site of a bridgehead being held by Major General Oscar W. Griswold's IV Corps. Included in General Griswold's forces as part of the Second Pursuit Wing was VMF-121's old Quantico mate, VMF-111.

The maneuvers proved valuable for both the U.S. Army and VMF-121. Lessons learned, like the many hours spent on navigational flights, more than proved their value when former VMF-121 pilots started flying combat missions.

The Blue Army "won" the battle against the Red Army when the maneuvers ended on 29 November. The Red air force had 360 planes

Captain Brackett signs off on a supply requistion while Tech Sergeant. J.W. Wolco and Phil Crawford look on. (R. Bruce Porter)

A trio of VMF-121 pilots pose in front of a Grumman F4F-3 on the flight line at New Bern. From left, L. Tolar Bryan, R. Bruce Porter and Phil Crawford. (Phil Crawford)

vs. the 320 aircraft of the Blue air force. A few of the squadron's pilots got to fly Army aircraft. One was Colonel Hamilton Lawrence, USMC, Ret. He recalled; *I got to fly (the Curtiss P-40) and did not like the airplane.*

The men of VMF-121 never quite got used to the very frigid weather conditions at Southern Pines. It was not much fun having to break the ice to wash your face in the morning or baring yourself to the icy air.

One of the most significant developments to come out of the 1941 GHQ maneuvers was the first operational use of pierced steel planking. The first use of this material came about on a grassy field near the town of Marston, N.C. Three-thousand feet of steel planking was laid down

Pilots "Jake" Baker, Phil Crawford and Hamilton Lawrence check out flight duty roster chalk board posted on the flight line at New Bern. (R. Bruce Porter)

on the field making it usable by the aircraft taking part in the exercise. Each plank was ten feet by fifteen inches, pierced by eighty-seven holes and weighed 66.2 pounds. They interlocked without the use of special tools and could be easily unassembled and moved for use at another site. This planking became known as "Marston Matting" and was used around the world during the Second World War. Some 36,000 planks were used on the field at Marston.

There were several incidents of a lighter nature during the time the squadron spent at Southern Pines. There was an "old fashioned" church supper being held in the vicinity of VMF-121's camp and squadron members Bud Stuckey, John Scallion and another Marine, decided to attend. It turned out that these three were the only Marines in attendance. There were, however, about twenty Army troops at the supper. The food was great; a country style covered dish, a nice change from the standard fare at Southern Pines. Following a brief church service, the attendees were treated to a show put on by the local residents. At the conclusion of the show, the Master of Ceremonies asked if anyone else wanted to add to the entertainment segment. The three Marines volunteered to sing the Marine Corps Hymn. They took the stage and struggled through the hymn. When they sang the words "If the Army and the Navy ever gaze on heaven's scene, they will find that they are guarded by United States Marines", a huge chorus of boos came forth from the Army attendees. The Army types, however, did not hold a grudge since they gave the three Marines who sang the hymn a lift back to camp.

Minor accidents made their way into the everyday activities of the squadron. Luckily none was more serious than when Pharron Cooke experienced a collapsed main landing gear while landing on the grass at Southern Pines. It was later determined that Sergeant Cooke's problem was directly attributed to his failure to lock the gear in the down position. His F4F-3, 121-F-6, suffered a bent propeller, but was back in the

2nd Lieutenant Wally Cloake in the cockpit of a Grumman F4F-3 at New Bern, North Carolina during the Fall of 1941. (Phil Crawford)

2nd Lieutenant Ken Chamberlain mans his F4F-3 while training at New Bern. (Phil Crawford)

2nd Lieutenant Tolar Bryan discusses some squadron business with the commanding officer, Major Jack, in the squadron tent city at New Bern. (L. Tolar Bryan)

2nd Lieutenants Bruce Porter and Tolar Bryan pose in front of an overall Light Gray F4F-3 Wildcat. From their uniforms, both men are probably getting ready to go to town on "liberty." (L. Toylar Bryan)

air within days.

The squadron had not been back at New Bern very long when the Japanese attacked Pearl Harbor on 7 December 1941. They immediately broke camp and moved to Quantico. There they worked around the clock installing self-sealing gas tanks and armor plate in their F4F's.

On 11 December, VMF-121 departed Quantico bound for San Diego and NAS North Island. Lieutenant Bruce Porter failed to get off due to a runaway propeller, but the rest of the squadron headed for their first stop at Florence, North Carolina. They took on fuel at Florence then headed to Charlotte, N.C. From there it was on to Montgomery, Alabama where they stayed for a day due to extremely bad enroute weather. On 13 December, the squadron took-off for Shreveport, Louisiana.

Bob Fraser, Bruce Porter and Tolar Bryan relax at the New Bern encampment between missions. Fraser, liked and respected by all, was killed on a routine flight off Santa Barbara, California on 18 June 1945. At the time, he was commander of Marine Carrier Air Group 7. (R. Bruce Porter)

2nd Lieutenant Tolar Bryan in the cockpit of his F4F-3, ready to begin another training mission. While at New Bern, the squadron maintained a heavy training schedule. (L. Toylar Bryan)

The next stop was NAS Dallas, Texas, where Bruce Porter caught up with the squadron. They had to spend an additional day waiting at Dallas for the weather to clear. On the way to Dallas, while passing over Louisiana, the senior 2nd Lieutenant in the squadron, Hamilton Lawrence, had a "run in" with a buzzard and damaged his Wildcat's wing. He and the rest of VMF-121 were flying at about 500 feet to stay out of the clouds.

After getting a late start out of Dallas, VMF-121 flew on to Midland, Texas. Then to El Paso. After El Paso, the squadron flew to Yuma, Arizona. It was near here that 1st Lieutenant Paul Ashley suffered an engine failure. He made a great approach to land on Highway 80 but met a car. When a wheel hit the shoulder of the road, he nosed-up, damaging the F4F's propeller.

They landed at Yuma and the ground crew, who had been following in an R3D-2, proceeded to change the propeller on Ashley's aircraft. He later took off from the highway and joined the rest of the squadron at NAS North Island.

On 16 December, the squadron arrived at NAS North Island, San Diego, California and got their first look at the Pacific Ocean. They were told that they had to go to the blimp mooring mast at Kearny Mesa where there was a 2,250 foot landing strip and nothing else. If you were

Major Sam Jack, commander of VMF-121, confers with two other pilots during a break between missions. (R. Bruce Porter)

Tech Sergeant Ken Walsh poses in front of one of the squadron's F4F-3s with his hand resting on one of the guns. If the ordnance chief caught him doing this, he would have let him know how he felt. The chief was very particular about the guns once they had been bore sighted. (Ken Walsh)

unlucky enough to wander off the runway, you would find your wheels up to their hubs in mud. This caused the squadron to land on one side of the runway and park their Wildcats on the other side.

The situation in the Pacific dictated the vital need to rush as many fighters to the area as possible to defend the Hawaiian Islands. On 26 December, VMF-121 and VMF-111 were informed that their F4F-3s were to be turned over to the pool for shipment to NAS Pearl Harbor in order to bring the fighter squadrons on the carriers up to full strength.

As replacements, VMF-121 ended up with a number of Brewster F2A-2 Buffalo fighters and trained with them from January to the first week of March. The Brewster was termed an *oil leaker and a mechanic's nightmare,* by squadron mechanic Bud Stuckey (Master Tech Sergeant,

Three Marine paratroopers from Camp Lejeune, North Carolina land at New Bern during a training jump. (Phil Crawford)

VMF-121's "night flyer," 2nd Lieutenant Phil Crawford during 1941. VMF-121 was his first unit, later he would command VMA-121 in Korea from 20 June to 10 September 1952. (Phil Crawford)

12-41) who worked on the Brewster fighter during this time period.

The only accident VMF-121 had with the Brewster F2A Buffalos during their two months with the squadron was a turn over by Pharron Cooke. The squadron flew a total of eight F2A-2s (BuNos 1411, 1413, 1416, 1417, 1422, 1424, 1430 and 1432) and at least one F2A-3 (BuNo 01596).

VMF-121 experienced quite a build-up at Kearney Mesa during the early months of 1942. They had been sharpening their flying skills with the F2A-2, however, the handwriting was already on the wall, so to speak, and additional expansion was well on the way. New Grumman F4F-4s began coming into the squadron during early March.

In accordance with the expected expansion, Marine Aircraft Group Twelve (MAG-12) was formed on 1 March 1942, with Captain John Condon in command. Condon had been Sam Jack's Executive Officer in the pre-war VMF-121 when the squadron was stationed at Quantico.

MAG-12 would soon give life to three more fighting squadrons, VMF-122, VMF-123 and VMF-124. VMF-121 personnel formed the nuclei of each of these new outfits. They also provided people for Headquarters Squadron Twelve.

Since VMF-121 provided the nucleus for the new squadrons, it was no

A Douglas R3D-2, side code 152-J-2, takes on a load of Marine parachute troops for a training jump at New Bern during 1941. The aircraft was overall Natural Metal with Black codes. (Phil Crawford)

11

A pair of Douglas R3D-2s of VMJ-152 in flight over the New Bern area. The Marines operated four of these transports, two in VMJ-152 and two in VMJ-252. The Navy also operated two R3D-1s and KLM flew the aircraft as the DC-5 on their Dutch East Indies route. None survive today. (USMC)

surprise to find a few familiar names in the Commanding Officer chairs of the newly formed squadrons. Captain Elmer E. Brackett, Jr., a pre-war VMF-121 Division Leader, now headed VMF-122. Lieutenant Cecil B. Brewer took over VMF-124. Even Sam Jack would make an

appearance, as commander of MAG-12, when he relieved John Condon. But he remained for only a short time. Things were on the move and VMF-121 was playing it's part.

The squadron's F4F-4s were now sporting the new high visibility markings which would change yet again by the time the squadron went into combat. The basic camouflage consisted of Non-specular Blue-Gray uppersurfaces over Non-specular Light Gray undersurfaces. The rudder was painted in alternating equal width stripes; seven Red with six in White. The national insignia was oversized and almost covered the whole of the wing chord. The fuselage insignia was oversized as well.

With the formation of MAG-12 on 1 March 1942, VMF-121 also

Major Jack's F4F-3 carries the White cross markings painted on the aircraft for the 1941 GHQ maneuvers at Southern Pines, North Carolina during November of 1941. The unit was assigned to the Blue Army. Tech Sergeant Leroy M. McCallum painted the crosses on the Wildcats in lacquer paint instead of water-based paint (as called for in the maneuver plan) so that the markings would stay on in the event of rain. (Leroy M. McCallum)

A North American O-47 observation aircraft of the 126th Observation Squadron, Wisconsin National Guard parked in a revetment during the GHQ maneuvers. VMF-121 shared the field with this unit. The aircraft also carried the White cross identification markings of the Blue Army, (Fred C. Dickey)

This Lockheed P-38D Lightning was attached to the Red Army during the Carolina manuevers. VMF-121 had their camp "strafed" by more than one of the Red forces P-38s. (USAAC)

A Bell P-39C Airacobra of the Red forces. It carried Red cross markings and a White band around the nose. (USAAC)

under went a reorganization. On that same day, the squadron was officially re-established with Major Leonard K. "Duke" Davis in command. Davis had flown with VMF-121 back in the pre-war days at New Bern. He was a 1935 graduate of the Naval Academy and well liked by almost everyone, even though he was very outspoken. The squadron Operations Officer, at that time, was another pre-war squadron member, 1st Lieutenant Eddie Fry.

The squadron continued training hard, since they knew it would only be a short time before they would be facing the Japanese. Personnel continued to flow through VMF-121 in the Spring and early Summer of 1942. It was as though they were a Marine Corps training squadron, which, it could be said, was technically true. By the time they did reach the combat zone, there were many new faces in the crowd.

One of those new faces came to VMF-121 on 1 August 1942, when 1st Lieutenant Joseph J. Foss reported to "Duke" Davis as Executive Officer of VMF-121 at Kearney Mesa.

On 7 August 1942, the Marines landed on the South Pacific island of Guadalcanal. The U.S. offensive phase had begun. Intelligence reports in the early Summer of 1942, had indicated that the Japanese were building an airfield near Lunga Point on the island of Guadalcanal in the Solomon Islands. This was the reason for the Marine landing. It was thought that once the Japanese established this airfield it would serve as an excellent stepping stone in their moves southward to threaten the flow of lifesaving aid to Australia and New Zealand that was coming from the United States.

The first Japanese move toward Australia came during the first week of May 1942. They had tried to take Port Moresby on the island of New Guinea, but were stopped by carrier aircraft from the USS LEXINGTON (CV-2) and USS YORKTOWN (CV-5). This action, 4 to 8 May, was the first time that two opposing forces never saw each other during

Army troops install Marston matting, also known as Pierced Steel Planking (PSP). This much needed development was used for the first time during the GHQ Carolina maneuvers in 1941. (U.S. Army)

the entire battle. The battle, which became known as the Battle of the Coral Sea, was fought by the carrier air groups.

The official code name for the Guadalcanal operation was Operation WATCHTOWER, but to anyone who set foot on the island, it would be better characterized as Operation SHOESTRING. This battle would be fought in a hot, humid and rainy environment so hostile that an inscription on a lone Marine's grave said it all, *"...and when he gets to heaven, to Saint Peter he will tell, one more Marine reporting sir; I've served my time in hell."*

On 7 August, VMF-121 was sixty-three days away from their Guadalcanal experience. By the afternoon of 8 August, the airfield on Guadalcanal was in Marine control. Almost immediately a Marine engineering battalion began finishing the almost completed airstrip. Before the week was over, the original 2,600 foot strip was expanded to 3,800 feet and ready for aircraft. On 12 August, the first U.S. aircraft landed on the airstrip, a PBY-5A Catalina flown by Lieutenant William S. Sampson, Admiral John S. McCain's aide.

A few days later the airfield was named in honor of Major Lofton R. Henderson, USMC. He had been lost while leading VMSB-241 against the Japanese Fleet at the Battle of Midway on 4 June 1942. Henderson Field was now ready for aircraft and on 20 August the first Marine aircraft landed on the airstrip.

VMF-223 with nineteen F4F-4s under the leadership of Captain John L. Smith and VMSB-232 with twelve Douglas SBD-3s under the command of Major Richard C. Mangrum were the first to arrive. They had flown off the escort carrier, USS LONG ISLAND (ACV-1). Escort carriers were originally designated as AVGs, changed to ACV in August of 1942 and finally to CVE in July of 1943.

Five pilots from VMF-121 preceded the rest of the squadron by fifteen days when they went ashore with Lieutenant Colonel Albert D. Cooley, commander of MAG-14. One of the pilots, 2nd Lieutenant George A. Treptow, became the first VMF-121 member lost to enemy action when he was listed as missing in action on 2 October. The pilots operated with VMF-223 and VMF-224 while awaiting the arrival of the rest of VMF-121. Eight of VMF-121s mechanics also came ashore.

On 1 September, VMF-121 sailed from San Diego aboard the troopship MATSONIA. Their F4Fs went out aboard the USS COPAHEE (ACV-12). On 29 September, the squadron reached the harbor of Noumea on the island of New Caledonia. It was here that they went aboard COPAHEE and practiced catapult launches, landing on the airfield at Tontouta on New Caledonia.

On 6 October, the squadron again embarked in USS COPAHEE and headed for the Solomon Islands. After three days on the little ship, VMF-121 strapped into their twenty F4F-4s to finally begin their three hour flight to Guadalcanal and the Second World War.

This was the landing ground at Camp Kearney Mesa, near San Diego, California. VMF-121 arrived here on 16 December 1941, to train while awaiting overseas assignment. (Phil Crawford)

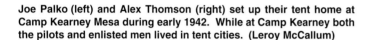

Joe Palko (left) and Alex Thomson (right) set up their tent home at Camp Kearney Mesa during early 1942. While at Camp Kearney both the pilots and enlisted men lived in tent cities. (Leroy McCallum)

VMF-121 flew the Brewster F2A-3 Buffalo fighter during January, February and early March of 1942, while awaiting delivery of their new F4F-4 Wildcats. Their F4F-3s had been sent to the Pacific to reinforce the carrier based fighter units. (Clay Jansson)

A pair of VMF-121 F4F-4s fly a tight combat spread formation during a training session near Kearney Mesa, in early 1942. (L. Tolar

Enlisted personnel kept up their miliatay drill training on the "grinder," even at places like Camp Kearney Mesa. Tolar Bryan, on the right, was in command of the drill. (L.Tolar Bryan)

Tech Sergeant Leroy McCallum (left) and Staff Sergeant W.C. Neuner relax with a gas powered model airplane at Kearney Mesa during May 1942. (W.H. Stuckey)

A F4F-4 Wildcat of VMF-121 comes in for a landing at Camp Kearney Mesa during July of 1942. The Red and White rudder stripes removed after a 15 May directive ordered their removal. The Red circle inside of White national insignia star was deleted at the same time. (Perry N. Coley via R.L. Lawson)

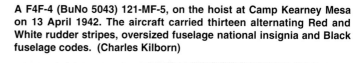

A F4F-4 (BuNo 5043) 121-MF-5, on the hoist at Camp Kearney Mesa on 13 April 1942. The aircraft carried thirteen alternating Red and White rudder stripes, oversized fuselage national insignia and Black fuselage codes. (Charles Kilborn)

(Right) 121-MF-6 running-up on the dirt strip at Camp Kearney Mesa during July of 1942, with the wheel chocks still in place. (Perry N. Coley via R.L. Lawson)

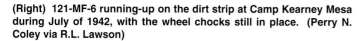

Squadron maintenance personnel work on the engine of 121-MF-4 (BuNo 5069) in a revetment at Kearney Mesa during July of 1942. The guns have been taped over to keep out dust and dirt. (Perry N. Coley via R.L. Lawson)

Ground crews button up 121-MF-4 for its next training hop. The aircraft was camouflaged in Non-specular Blue-Gray on the uppersurfaces, with Non-specular Light Gray on the undersurfaces. (Perry N. Coley via R.L. Lawson)

This wheels-up landing was no doubt caused by the pilot's failure to turn the landing gear crank the full twenty-eight turns that it took to lower the wheels and lock them in place. 121-MF-3 was soon repaired and was back in the air a short time after the mishap. (Perry N. Coley via R.L. Lawson)

A squadron mechanic really "into his work" on this F4F-4 at Kearney Mesa during July of 1942. The aircraft is chocked and tied down and has a protective cover in place over the engine. (Perry N. Coley via R.L. Lawson)

Squadron personnel undergo the time honored crossing the Equator initiation aboard SS MATSONIA on 8 September 1942. The men of VMF-121 then joined the proud ranks of "Shellbacks" (all those who have sailed across the Equator). (Tom Mann)

The SS MATSONIA and SS LURLINE enroute to the South Pacific. Personnel from VMF-121 embarked aboard the two ships in San Diego on 1 September 1942 and arrived at Somoa on Monday, 14 September 1942. They then traveled to Noumea, New Caledonia, arriving on 23 September 1942. (Tom Mann)

The squadron's F4Fs were transported to the combat area aboard the escort carrier USS COPAHEE, ACV-12. She was similar to this escort carrier (USS CHARGER, CVE-30). (USN)

Guadalcanal

By the time the squadron arrived, there were several VMF-121 pilots already on Guadalcanal. The pilots coming in from USS COPAHEE were proceeded by the advance echelon that arrived on 25 September 1942. These included; 2nd Lieutenants Thomas H. Mann, Jr., John S.P. Dean, Floyd A. Lynch, Jacob A.O. Stub, and George A. Treptow. Eight mechanics also arrived on the same day including Donzel D. Alley, Nicholas Boris, James W. Burns, Orville Busekrus, Charles W. Edwards, Edward L. Foilis, Robert L. Irby with Wilbur H. "Bud" Stuckey, NCOIC (Non-Commissioned Officer In Charge) in charge. On 6 October, Master Technical Sergeants Joe Palko - NAP and Alexander Thomson - NAP arrived to join the advance team.

On 8 October, nine more VMF-121 pilots came into Henderson Field. These included 2nd Lieutenants David K. Allen, Samuel B. Folsom, Hugo A. Olsson, Jr., Roy M. A. Ruddell, Edward P. Andrews, Donald L. Clark, Lowell D. Grow, Frank H. Presley and Paul S. Rutledge. They were followed on 10 October by Staff Sergeant James A. Feliton - NAP

Welcome to Henderson Field. This is the view of the field looking north with Iron Bottom Sound beyond the jungle. The "Pagoda," at the left center, served as the operations center for Guadalcanal's air operations during the first months of the battle. (National Archives)

The first aircraft to land on Guadalcanal on 12 August 1942 was this PBY-5A flown by Lieutenant William S. Sampson, aide to Vice Admiral John S. McCain. It took off later that day with a load of wounded Marines. (USMC)

The "Pagoda" was built by the Japanese and used for a while as the operations building. It was later bulldozed by the Seebees, since Major General Roy S. Geiger, Commanding General, 1st Marine Aircraft Wing, felt that the building made an ideal aiming point for Japanese gunners. (USMC)

and 2nd Lieutenants Oscar M. Bate, Jr. and Donald G. Owen.

Henderson Field now had VMF-121 pilots aboard with seventeen more to follow.

"At the beginning of the war the Japanese naval pilot training program was reasonably well stabilized. Prospective pilots were given from six months to two and a half years of pre-flight training depending on their previous experience and education. The pre-flight work consisted of a thorough military indoctrination, general academic courses particularly in basic mathematics and physics and in ordinary ground school subjects. There was no flying during this period. Those chosen from the pre-flight schools as pilot material were sent to primary training units for six months, during which they amassed a total of about seventy flying hours, soloing in about twelve hours.

Upon graduation from primary the trainee entered an intermediate training period of about five months in length with perhaps fifty to sixty hours of flight.

During the advanced stage of pilot training, the Japanese Navy pilot ordinarily flew the combat type he would later use in actual combat. At the end of that advanced training, when the pilot received his wings, he would join an operational training group. These groups were located within the Empire, in the early stages of the war, and while in them the aviator would usually compile quite an impressive flight log. In the beginning, a pilot in an active combat area might be expected to have between 1,500 and 4,000 flight hours.

The early policy lightly regarded the life of the pilot, who was often referred to as a "human bullet," considered the Bushido spirit as of greater significance than the parachute, and looked with a mixture of amazement and scorn upon Allied efforts to rescue pilots downed in the

One of the advanced echelon's tents on Guadalcanal. 2nd Lieutenant Jacob A. O. Stub looks out from the tent while another Marine uses the makeshift latrine. (Tom Mann)

2nd Lieutenant Thomas H. Mann relaxes at the table used by the pilots at night when they gathered for their one drink ration after the days operations. (Tom Mann)

Solomon Islands area. This policy cost the Japanese Navy a great percentage of its pre-war pilots." (United States Pacific Fleet and Pacific Ocean Areas Weekly Intelligence Report, Volume 1, Number 14, 13 October 1944.)

This report, written two years after the Guadalcanal experience, most likely provided a somewhat accurate picture of the men facing the Marines during the struggle for that island. Certainly the Japanese Navy pilots at Coral Sea and Midway were high flight time aviators and it could be said that the same held true for the pilots engaged at Guadalcanal.

Considering the experience of the Japanese pilots flying against our Naval Aviators during the Solomons campaign, one has to be very impressed with the performance exhibited by our Marine and Navy pilots. Most of these young men were fresh out of flight training, yet they defeated the best the Japanese could put into the air. During the early stages of the Solomon Islands campaign, 2.5 Japanese aircraft were shot down for every Navy or Marine aircraft lost to enemy action. This ratio continued to expand until the end of the war, in our favor.

On Friday, 9 October, the last element of VMF-121 pilots flew into Henderson Field. The flight, led by the squadron commander, Major Leonard K. Davis, consisted of the following pilots: Captain Joseph J. Foss - Squadron Executive Officer, 1st Lieutenants Otto H. Brueggeman, Jr., Edwin C. Fry, Gregory M. Loesch, 2nd Lieutenants Koller C. Brandon, John W. Clark Wiley H. Craft, Cecil J. Doyle, William B. Freeman, Thomas W. Furlow, Roger A.Haberman, Joseph L. Narr, Arthur N. Nehf, Jr., John E. Schuler, Wallace G. Wethe, William P. Marontate. VMF-121 arrived on Guadalcanal one pilot short, 2nd Lieutenant Robert F. Simpson had crashed on take off from USS COPAHEE, but was successfully rescued.

To some, first impressions are very important and the impression made by Henderson Field on VMF-121's personnel was somewhat subdued. The squadron landed on the main runway which was just a dirt strip bulldozed out of the heavy jungle growth and covered with

Wildcats are parked far apart on the flight line at Fighter One, the main fighter field on Guadalcanal. (Tom Mann)

Marines gather in the "bathtub" on Guadalcanal. (Tom Mann)

Marston matting. They were almost immediately met by scores of officers and enlisted men, very happy to see more fighters and fighter pilots on the island.

Of course, the celebration proved to be of a rather short duration when they were greeted by the skipper of VMF-223, Major John L. Smith, who told them they had landed on the wrong runway. He then directed them to the correct strip, which was about a mile away. The squadron wasted little time in taking off and heading for the correct landing strip. On landing, Major Davis found that the squadron had already suffered its first loss. 2nd Lieutenant George A, Treptow, had been killed on 2 October while flying with VMF-223.

As of 10 October, VMF-121 had thirty-five officers and twenty-five enlisted men on its roster. This was the day that the unit flew its first combat mission. Major Davis led Captain Foss, 1st Lieutenant Fry, 2nd Lieutenants Furlow, Rutledge, Nehf, Narr, Loesch, Doyle, Marontate, Brandon and Master Technical Sergeant Joseph J. Palko on a mission escorting nine SBD-3s against Japanese surface vessels operating in the Slot, the thin stretch of ocean between Guadalcanal and New Georgia (to the southeast) and Santa Isabel and the Choiseul Islands (to the Northwest). One enemy destroyer was hit, but no enemy aircraft opposed the mission and all Marine aircraft returned safely.

Guadalcanal quickly adopted the code name "Cactus" and a short time later VMF-223 and VMSB-232 began to call themselves the Cactus Air Force. The name stuck and VMF-121 also began to use the term.

By 11 October, VMF-121 had added 110 enlisted men to the squadron. Officer strength was also bolstered by three.

Maintenance of the squadron's F4F-4s on Henderson Field was a matter of both skill and luck. The squadron mechanics had more than enough skill, the luck factor came into play when it came to obtaining the necessary parts to repair 121's aircraft. All aircraft parts were controlled by the Aviation Quartermaster (AQ) on Henderson Field. On

A F4F-4 of VMF-121 rolling down Marston matting toward the take-off strip on Henderson Field. The aircraft has a forty-two gallon, centerline auxiliary fuel tank which was not a popular item with 121's pilots. These tanks had a tendency to "hang-up" when the pilot wanted to jettison them prior to an engagement. (Perry N. Coley via R.L. Lawson)

Two of the squadron's Wildcats roar down the runway on Henderson Field's Fighter One airstrip as VMF-121 scrambles to intercept incoming Japanese aircraft during October of 1942. (Tom Mann)

A F4F-4 Wildcat, equipped with one of the centerline fuel tanks, rolls out for take-off during November of 1942. The second aircraft in the line has a single underwing fuel tank, which was much more popular with the crews. (Perry N. Coley via R.L. Lawson)

many occasions mechanics would go to the AQ for a particular part and find SBD parts mixed in with F4F parts and the quartermaster personnel would not know the difference. They would hunt around for awhile and then become so confused that they would say they did not have the part. Finally, in desperation, the 121 mechs would go through the stock bins themselves and find the part they needed. This was not an ideal situation, but it was reality and those involved did the best they could. Living conditions were extremely crude, they were under constant threat of Japanese attack and they were operating with the bare necessities. To say that times were tough would be an understatement.

Keeping the squadron's F4Fs flying meant paying attention to little things. The climate of the area was especially rough on rubber parts such as hoses, tail wheels, grommetts, etc. Dust fouled fuel pressure diaphragms, blower and cooler parts. When it rained, the soggy field conditions took their toll on propellers, wings and landing gear parts. Wet weather brought about many operational accidents on the field.

This F4F-4 of VMF-121 was equipped with a fifty-eight gallon external fuel tank under its starboard (right) wing. It was the usual routine to fly a mission with only one tank hung on the wing. (Perry N. Coley via R.L. Lawson)

On the F4F, the oil coolers were constantly being shot. This would cause an oil leak and debris would get into the engine and ruin it. Oil coolers and engines went hand in hand, when the mechanics changed one, the other also had to be changed. Sometimes they would flush out an oil cooler and get by with it, but it was dangerous and only done as a last ditch operation. The conditions faced by everyone on the island in the early days of the fighting were not even imaginable, just nine months before the Guadalcanal battle.

In VMF-121, the men responsible for much of the organization that made it possible for the squadron's mechanics to operate efficiently were the Assistant to the Commander for Material, 1st Lieutenant Henry O. DeFries, Engineering Chief - Master Technical Sergeant Harold Sobol and Master Technical Sergeant Parker V.S. Reed, the squadron's Ordnance Chief.

Sergeant Francis J. Mayer, master metalsmith, played a very important role in keeping the squadron's F4Fs in the air. Mayer had served in the Army from June of 1938 until June of 1941. He soldiered with the 6th Field Artillery at Fort Hoyle, Maryland. At the time, the 6th was utilizing horse drawn cassons bearing French 75mm guns. He quickly moved up through the enlisted ranks and had achieved the rank of Sergeant, Battery B, chief of the 2nd section, gunnery sergeant. Upon our entry into the Second World War, Mayer was offered a commission in the Army but elected to enlist in the Marine Corps as a Private.

The Marine Corps made a metalsmith out of him and the same dedication he displayed while with the Army, came to the fore and the Army's

A F4F-4, No. 20, of VMF-121 lands on Fighter One during November of 1942. According to Tom Mann, this was either Captain Joe Foss or Major "Duke" Davis, Commading Officer of 121. The Wildcat's flaps are fully extended indicating the F4Fs vacuum tank escaped enemy fire during the flight. The tank, located behind the pilot, was very vulnerable in combat and was often disabled during a fight. The mechanics patched the tanks with dope and fabric. (Tom Mann)

squadron's aircraft and Meyer would more than make the most of his time. He would get into the squadron jeep with his Engineering Officer, and they would inspect the Wildcats after every flight and he would tell Lieutenant DeFries how long it would take to repair each fighter. He also told him what had to be done to each. DeFries would then decide which to work on first, which to save and which to scrap. Mayer would work through shellings and bombings and on one occasion he worked until 0100 in a driving rain to complete a job so that the Wildcat would be ready the next day. He did jobs that others said could not be done and earned the respect and admiration of his superiors during those very difficult early months of the Guadalcanal operation. All maintenance personnel on the island earned the pilots undying respect each and every

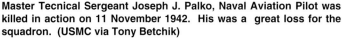

Master Tecnical Sergeant Joseph J. Palko, Naval Aviation Pilot was killed in action on 11 November 1942. His was a great loss for the squadron. (USMC via Tony Betchik)

loss became the Marine Corps' gain. He once built four feet of wing for an R4D that had ground looped. The pilot later remarked that it was as good as the original.

Time and serviceability were the main factors in maintaining the

Bell P-400 fighters attached to the 67th Pursuit Squadron, USAAF. The P-400 was the British version of the U.S. Army's P-39 Airacobra fighter. The pilots of this squadron flew alongside VMF-121 during the Guadalcanal campaign. On 14 September 1942, three P-400s of the 67th took-off in support of the Marines on Lunga Ridge. They fought until they ran out of ammunition, but they saved the day for the Marines. Captain John A. Thompson won the Navy Cross for his actions. (Robert J. Cressman Collection)

2nd Lieutenant Thomas H. Mann poses alongside his F4F-4 at Fighter One on Guadalcanal during November of 1942. The individual aircraft number was 6 and the aircraft carried eight Japanese flag kill markings under the cockpit. (Tom Mann)

day.

VMF-121 spent a somewhat restful first night on the island, but, to the West, the Japanese were busy landing more troops on the island. On the morning of 11 October, patrols started going up at approximately 0930. No contacts were made and the flight returned safely to Henderson Field. At 1230 the order to scramble rang out loud and clear. The squadron put thirteen F4Fs into the air and headed for the incoming Japanese flight. The enemy had sent a force of some twenty-eight bombers accompanied by almost as many Zero fighters. It was on this mission that 2nd Lieutenant Nehf was shot down. He landed in the ocean, injuring his eye. All other squadron aircraft returned safely.

Major Robert E. Galer's VMF-224 had accounted for four Zeros and seven bombers. A number pilots from VMF-223 shared in another bomber. A P-400 pilot from the 67th Pursuit Squadron also shot down another. This unit had been on Guadalcanal since 22 August and was flying the export variant of the P-39, the P-400.

Often passed over in recognition of their contribution to the struggle on Guadalcanal, the 67th Pursuit Squadron was flying these "rejects" from the RAF, the P-400. This aircraft had a 20MM cannon that fired through the propeller spinner in place of the larger 37MM weapon fitted to the P-39. It also carried two .50 caliber and four .30 caliber machine guns. In addition, it was also able to carry a bomb on a centerline rack

F4F-4s parked on Fighter One, Guadalcanal during November of 1942, while a flight of Army B-17s pass overhead. (USMC)

An Army P-400 taxis out for a ground support mission with a 500 pound bomb on the under fuselage bomb rack. (Tom Mann)

located under the fuselage. The P-400s were equipped with a high pressure oxygen system, as per British requirements, but supplies of that product soon became extinct. This limited the P-400 pilots to flying at approximately twelve to fourteen thousand feet. As a result, it was used mainly in the ground support role.

The 67th soldiered on alongside the Marines, their finest hour was probably the desperate battle of Bloody Ridge on 14 September. This occurred very near to Henderson Field when the Japanese launched a vicious attack at Lunga Ridge just south of the airstrip. The Marine Raiders and Paramarines fought all night long, at times losing ground but then regaining it. Only the inner perimeter stood between the Japanese and Henderson Field.

Shortly before 0730, the three remaining flyable P-400s were put into air to fly in support of the Marines on Lunga Ridge. Captain John A. Thompson, 1st Lieutenant B.W. Brown and 2nd Lieutenant B.E. Davis were the pilots that flew the mission. They made pass after pass against the Japanese and finally small arms fire had its effect, damaging two of the P-400s. These had to make dead stick landings on Henderson Field. The third P-400, flown by Captain Thompson, flew on until his ammunition was exhausted.

The ridge was secured by the Marines, thanks in part to the 67th's three P-400s. Marine Major General Alexander A. Vandegrift, 1st Marine Division commanding general, remarked that the three P-400s saved Guadalcanal that particular day. Captain Thompson was recommended for the Navy Cross by General Vandegrift, while Brown and Davis, were recommended for the Silver Star. In due time they were all decorated.

Tuesday, 13 October was a day to remember for everyone located at or near Henderson Field. Japanese bombers were almost over the island before the fighter squadrons got into the air. There had been a communications failure and warning of the fast approaching bombers and fighters was delayed.

The enemy hit Henderson Field, causing heavy damage to the airstrip's Marston matting and to several Army B-17s parked adjacent to the runway. This attack, which began at approximately noon, also suc-

This Lockheed P-38F Lightning was assigned to the Army's 339th Fighter Squadron which shared Henderson Field with the Marines. (Tom Mann)

Flight crews of VMF-121 conferring with Lieutenant Colonel Harold W. Bauer near the squadron ready tent on Henderson Field during October of 1942. (from Left) 2nd Lieutenant Roger A. Haberman (back to camera), Major Paul J. Fontana (VMF-112), Captain Joe Foss (back to camera), Lieutenant Colonel Bauer, Major "Duke" Davis, 2nd Lieutenant William P. Marontate, 2nd Lieutenant Tom Mann (behind Davis) with 2nd Lieutenant Bob Simpson and Staff Sergeant James A. Feliton, Naval Aviation Pilot (NAP). (Tom Mann)

2nd Lieutenant John E. Schuler also came into Henderson Field with the 9 October 1942 flight and was later based at Faleola, Western Samoa during February of 1943. (John E. Schuler)

A "Ready Room" discussion after a successful flight. (From Left) 2nd Lieutenant John E. Schuler, Master Tech Sergeant Joe Palko, 2nd Lieutenant Cecil J. Doyle, Captain Joe Foss and Major Davis. (Tom Mann)

2nd Lieutenant Arthur N. Nehf, Jr., came into Henderson Field with the 9 October 1942 flight with "Duke" Davis leading the way. He was later based at Faleola, Western Samoa during February of 1943. (John E. Schuler)

ceeded in destroying some 5,000 gallons of badly needed aviation fuel for the aircraft stationed at Henderson.

VMF-121 put twenty-three F4Fs into the air during that first raid. Joe Narr shot down one Zero, while 2nd Lieutenant Bill Freeman accounted for another. All 121 aircraft returned safely with the exception of Lieutenant Narr, who landed in the ocean because of mechanical failure. He was picked up by Higgins boat and returned to the squadron that same day, ready to fly again.

The remaining fighters of VMF-121 had landed and were in the

2nd Lieutenant Walace G. Wephe was another pilot who came into Henderson Field with the 9 October 1942 flight. Like the others he also went to Faleola, Western Samoa in February of 1943. (John E. Schuler)

A Henderson Field based F4F-4 churns up dust on take-off from Fighter One. "Bud" Stuckey's remembers Captain Joe Foss in his F4F during a similiar situation. "With an unlit cigar stub in his mouth, I can picture him now, alertly peering over his gunsight, as he sped down the runway." This F4F shows the wear and tear of operational life on Guadalcanal. (USMC)

process of being refueled when the Japanese again approached the island. VMF-121 managed to get ten F4Fs into the air to oppose the fifteen bombers and ten fighters bent on causing more damage to Henderson Field. It was on this flight that Captain Joe Foss shot down his first Japanese aircraft, a Zero. He barely made it back to Henderson Field, as he was attacked by three Zeros after scoring his first kill. His F4F was badly shot up and he had to make a dead stick landing back on Henderson. He had made it, but it had been close. The Bettys and Zeros the squadron fought so hard to turn back, managed to bomb the airfield but inflicted only minor damage. Two more flights, one at 1520 and another at 1650 were made that day, but no contacts were made and all aircraft returned safely.

The night of 13 October was fast approaching as were the Japanese battleships KONGO and HARUMA, along with assorted cruisers and destroyers. The bombardment was close at hand. According to the VMF-121 War Diary, the preliminaries began about 2200. The squadron had already been under a blackout order, but had not yet left the confines of their tents, located near the airfield. The Japanese had landed numerous field pieces a couple of days earlier. While this caused

SBDs, TBFs, PBYs and at least one Army B-17 on the flight line at Henderson Field, Guadalcanal during 1942. (USMC)

Samuel B. Folsom made Captain while the squadron was at Faleola, Western Samoa in 1943. He was a 2nd Lieutennat while flying from Fighter One on Guadalcanal. He arrived on the island on 8 October 1942. (John E. Schuler)

Another Guadalcanal veteran, 2nd Lieutenant Donald L. Clark also made Captain on Faleola, Western Samoa during 1943. (John E. Schuler)

24

Captain Joe Foss chats with two Navy ordnancemen loading ammunition boxes for F4Fs on the flight line at Henderson Field. Foss became the leading Marine ace of the Guadalcanal period with a total of twenty-six kills. (Grumman)

Major Jack Cram made daring attack with a PBY Catalina against Japanese shipping on 15 October 1942. (USMC via Tony Betchik)

some concern, it was not worth laying in a foxhole or slit trench all night. Events began slowly and minimal damage was inflicted upon the airstrip and surrounding areas, by the sporadic shelling. A few enemy aircraft flew over Henderson Field but caused no major concern.

Flares lit up parts of the island and the intermittent shelling continued. Shortly after 0130, one or more Japanese aircraft flew in over Henderson Field and began dropping colored flares. A Red one over the west end of the airstrip, a White one over the middle and a Green one over the east end. That seemed to be the signal for the off-shore Japanese fleet, which included the KONGO and HARUNA, to begin the heaviest bombardment ever visited on them up to that time.

Shells from the sixteen fourteen inch guns of the combined battleships rained down on Henderson Field and the surrounding coconut groves that provided living space for the pilots of the Cactus Air Force. VMF-121's personnel spent the next hour or so, hugging the ground in the fox-

Marines use CO2 extinguishers to put out the fire in this F4F-4, which was damaged by Japanese shell fire. (USMC)

holes they had dug shortly after their arrival.

The big shells, over 900 hit the area, did a great deal of damage. Only one third of these shells were high-explosive projectiles; this type caused most of the damage. When they detonated, they sent sharp pieces of shrapnel in all directions, cutting down everything in it's path. Palm trees, buildings, aircraft and people suffered under the onslaught of this type of shell. The rest of the big battleship's shells were of the armor-piercing variety. When these shells hit, the result was one huge hole in the ground.

The worst of the bombardment was over by 0230. The Japanese had really made an impression on Henderson Field with some forty-one men being killed during the shelling. The squadron that suffered the most was VMSB-141, an SBD unit commanded by Major Gordon A. Bell. Major Bell, his Executive Officer, Captain R.A. Abbott and his Flight Officer, Captain E.F. Miller and two of his pilots, 2nd Lieutenants

VMF-121 pilots confer in the ready tent. (From left) 1st Lieutenant Lawrence M. Faulkner (in chair, VMF-212), 2nd Lieutenant Roger Haberman, 2nd Lieutenant Roy M.A. Ruddell (leaning on tree), Major Paul Fontana (standing, VMF112 CO), 1st Lieutenant Ben Finney, 2nd Lieutenant Joe Narr, 1st Lieutenant Frank C. Drury (VMF-212), Major Duke Davis, 1st Lieutenant Gred K. Loesch and 2nd Lieutenant Jacob A. O. Stub. (Tom Mann)

25

Two VMF-121 pilots in the unit's "trusty old Jeep." (From Left) 1st Lieutenant Eddie Fry, 2nd Lieutenant Bob Simpson and Major Robert E. Galer, Commanding Officer of VMF-224. (Tom Mann)

Major Davis and Lieutenant Finney look at the "last bottle of lucky booze" on Guadalcanal. (Tom Mann)

Henry F. Chaney, Jr. and George L. Haley, were lost in the attack.

Just about all of Guadalcanal's aviation gasoline went up in flames. The Marston matting was twisted and torn apart and thirty-five SBDs were unflyable. Of the eight Army B-17s on the field, two were destroyed. Only six of the Army's fighters could be flown. Most of the Grumman TBF-1s were damaged and not airworthy. With all the shells that slammed into the Henderson Field area, the fighter strip escaped with only minor damage and the hard working mechanics of VMF-121 managed to get sixteen F4Fs ready for flight by 0950 on the morning of 14 October. No contacts were made and all pilots returned safely.

The fuel situation took a turn for the better when about 400 drums of 100 octane aviation gasoline was discovered hidden in the nooks and crannies of the area surrounding Henderson Field. The fuel, stored earlier by Lieutenant Colonel Woods, had been all but forgotten. Luckily, one of Brigadier General Roy S. Geiger's aides remembered that Woods had hidden the fuel. The fuel problem, for the next couple of days, had eased.

At noon on 14 October, the Japanese again sent a flight of Betty bombers over Henderson Field. Little damage was done this time around. Not too long after this flight, the Japanese sent another eighteen bombers escorted by Zero fighters. VMF-121, together with members of VMF-224 and VF-5 (a Navy unit), scrambled twelve F4F-4s. Joe Foss shot down one Zero fighter and an enlisted pilot, Master Technical Sergeant Joe Palko shot down one of the Bettys. During the engagement, 2nd Lieutenant Koller C. Brandon was shot down. 14 October

A ground crewman rests in the shade under the wing of a VMF-121 F4F-4 parked on Henderson Field's Fighter One during November of 1942. (Tom Mann)

turned out to be a dark day for VMF-121. On the second scramble of the day, 2nd Lieutenant Paul S. Rutledge was lost to Japanese anti-aircraft fire while escorting SBD dive bombers on a mission to strafe and bomb a Japanese convoy. On the last flight of the day, Tech Sergeant Alexander Thomson was lost when his F4F experienced mechanical failure. Thomson had been a pre-war member of VMF-121.

The Tokyo Express paid another visit to Henderson Field that night. This time they only lobbed 752 eight inch shells into the area. This action also failed to halt operations on the airstrip.

More fighter pilots came aboard Henderson on 16 October when Lieutenant Colonel Harold W. Bauer brought in his squadron, VMF-212, with sixteen F4Fs. They were assigned to VMF-121 on Special Temporary Aviation Duty (STAD) as of that date. Other STAD pilots joining in with 121 were Lieutenant Carl C. Rooney, Lieutenant (JGs) Millard C. Thrash, Harold Reese, Roland Kenton and Ensign Norman V. Brown. All these pilots were from VF-71 aboard USS WASP (CV-7) which had been lost on 15 September. They also welcomed Tech Sergeant Emmet L. Anderson of VMO-251 also assigned on STAD (the VMF-121 War Diary uses the designation "VMF" when referencing 251. The unit was commissioned on 1 December 1941, as "VMO-251" and did not officially change to VMF-251 until 15 January 1945.)

Bauer's VMF-212 arrived on the scene during an enemy air raid. VMF-121 had put eleven planes into the air to help counter the Japanese bombing attack which had started at about 1645. The bombers had begun the raid by attacking our ships off shore. One ship, the USS McFARLAND (DD-237), had been hit that afternoon during this attack. Earlier in the day, the McFARLAND had delivered some 40,000 gallons of much needed aviation fuel. She had been classified as an AVD, sea-

Sergeant Nicholas Boris peers out of the baggage compartment hatch on a F4F. (John Rohrback)

F4Fs line the runway at Fighter Two on Guadalcanal during late 1942. Fighter Two was located two miles Northwest of Fighter One. (Grumman)

plane tender, earlier in her career and had the ability to transport large quantities of fuel. At the time of the attack she had been transporting some 160 hospital cases and of these, twenty-seven were killed in the raid.

VMF-212 had just been called up from Efate (coded "Roses" ["Roses" - Efate, "Buttons" - Espiritu Santos, "White Poppy" - Noumea]). During this engagement, Lieutenant Colonel Bauer shot down four Japanese Val dive bombers. This earned him the Medal of Honor, but he never lived to see the award. He was lost in action on 14 November.

By this time, the aviation gasoline situation on Guadalcanal was beginning to improve. Douglas R4D-1s (C-47s) of VMJ-253 brought in fuel on a regular basis and more and more ships of all kinds were adding their loads to the inventory.

Not too far from the 121 campsite was the Quonset hut that served both as the hospital and mess hall. The mess hall being one third of the facility. On Guadalcanal everyone's second enemy was diarrhea or malaria. This, combined with many sleepless nights plus the hot and humid weather, took a heavy toll on men already living under almost unbearable conditions. Their diet of luncheon meat (the ever popular Spam), Vienna sausage, corned beef, powdered eggs and dehydrated potatoes, would not be found at the Top of the Mark or at the Brown Derby. Needless to say, the hospital was never at a loss for patients. The Flight Surgeons on the island performed an outstanding service.

Two of the best were Lieutenant Henry R. Ringness and Lieutenant Victor S. Falk. Lieutenant Ringness administered to the many wounded Marines on the night of the big bombardment even though he had been paralyzed during the attack. Doctor Falk cared for the wounded after the 13/14 October shelling by going without sleep or food for a forty-eight hour period as he served as a doctor, ambulance driver and surgeon. He received the Silver Star for his dedication to duty. Lieutenant Ringness died three days after the shelling and received his award posthumously.

Shelling continued against the war weary Marines, soldiers and sailors on Guadalcanal for what seemed to be forever. On top of the shelling were the nightly visits from "Washing Machine Charlie", who dropped his small bombs hither-thither and yon. The field piece that shelled the field on a regular basis came to be known as "Pistol Pete." This heavy artillery battery, located beyond the Matanikau River, kept up a daily harassment of the field. This was the way it was and everyone did the best they could under the circumstances.

One innovative idea that helped to ease the pain during that dark October was the torpedo attack made by Major Jack Cram, General Geiger's personal pilot. The Japanese thought that the bombardment of 13/14 October had achieved exactly what they wanted - annihilation of our air power on Guadalcanal. True, things were not very good at that point, but we were not out.

An enemy convoy was headed toward the island loaded with troops and supplies, in broad daylight. Major Cram asked for and received permission to hang two aerial torpedoes, one under each wing of Geiger's PBY-5A Catalina. He then proceeded to take-off and hoped to con-

A lighter moment for some of the VMF-121 ground crews and mechanics on Guadalcanal. (From Left) Sergeant Nick Boris, Private First Class Irvin R. Zivney, Sergeant Charles W. Edwards and Corporal John R. Hrisak. (John Rohrback)

tribute to the demise of one of the Japanese ships steaming for Guadalcanal.

Cram and his five man crew soon spotted the enemy and the Major began his long dive. He had set his sight on a lumbering transport and headed straight for it. He then pulled the release handles and hoped for the best. Of the two torpedoes, one hit home and the other missed. He then turned quickly and headed for Henderson Field. By now his "Blue Goose" was receiving attention from a number of Zero fighters. One Zero pilot kept coming, even over Henderson Field. One VMF-121 pilot, 2nd Lieutenant Roger A. Haberman. saw Cram coming over the field with four Zeros chasing him. Haberman was flying at approximately 2,500 feet, so he had a slight altitude advantage. The VMF-121 pilot picked out one of the Zeros and sprayed him with gunfire. The Zero turned out to sea and exploded. Cram by now was well on his way to Henderson Field's landing strip. Realizing that he could not catch-up to the other Zeros, who were on their way home, Haberman lowered the wheels of his F4F and landed.

Of the many holes in both Cram's PBY and Haberman's F4F, all who were present that day think some of them must have come from friendly fire. There were so many tracers streaking across the sky in the general direction of all three planes, that some surely had to hit the PBY and F4F. Jack Cram was awarded the Navy Cross for his actions that day.

Mention must be made of the outstanding rescue work performed by the Marines who flew the low and slow Grumman J2F-5 Ducks. Many a Solomon's area pilot and aircrewman owes his life to the fine work performed by the pilots of these old pre-war biplanes. Although called

This beat-up and used-up F4F-4 of VMF-121 was used as a "hangar Queen" a source of spare parts for other F4Fs on Guadalcanal. (Tom Mann)

Corporal Tony Betchik smiles for the camera during routine engine work on a F4F-4 of VMF-121 on Guadalcanal during 1942. (John Rohrback)

the Duck by the Navy, it was often referred to as the "Shoehorn" by those who worked with it.

Henderson Field continued to come under attack from what seemed to be flight after flight of Japanese bombers and fighters coming down from their bases on Rabaul and Kavieng to the northwest. 17 October provided many in the squadron the opportunity to rid the skies of enemy planes. "Duke" Davis, Roger Haberman, Greg Loesch, Joe Narr and Wally Wethe accounted for eight Betty bombers with Bill Freeman bringing down two Zero fighters.

The next day, 18 October, Captain Joe Foss became an Ace when he shot down his fifth Japanese plane. VMF-121's 2nd Lieutenant Thomas H. Mann, Jr., also received credit for half a Zero on this flight, sharing it with VF-71's Ensign Norm Brown. Lieutenant Mann would later distinguish himself by downing four Japanese bombers during one combat engagement. This same day, VMF-121 lost one of its pilots to a take-off accident while scrambling to head off an incoming flight of Japanese bombers.

The condition "Yellow" alert was issued and word had come in that three waves of bombers were coming in and were about 117 miles out. Information followed that there were forty-five bombers with an escort of Zeros. At this time the Red flag went up the pole.

The mechanics had all the F4Fs ready for flight. They were all gassed-up, the propellers, mags, engines and tabs had been checked. The pilots came rushing out to the fighters; the jeeps fairly flew over the ground as they dropped each pilot at his designated F4F, which had been idling in anticipation of his arrival.

A pair of F4F Wildcats stand alert on Fighter One. (Tom Mann

Once the pilots had been assisted into and strapped in the cockpit, they taxied to the west end of the field for take-off. From all sides could be heard the powerful roar of the F4F's Pratt & Whitney engines as they started their take-off rolls. First by one and then by two.

Heavy torrential rains had fallen during the past two days, although sporadically since the Monsoon season had not quite begun. The resultant mud and silt combined with the softness of the field itself, had hampered take-offs in several instances. This usually happened early in the day, for when the sun rose, its scorching rays would dry even the wettest spots in very short order. The relentless heat had completely dried-up the area and as the fighters rushed over the ground, they raised huge clouds of dust. It was most severe at the starting line. One F4F mechanic, Private First Class Anthony J. Betchik wondered aloud, "How the hell can they see?"

One F4F surged forward on the port side of the runway in Betchik's direction. The armorers were still working on the F4F ahead of Betchik's Wildcat. The plane captain, Corporal James W. Curlee, was sitting under the wing waiting for armorers, Corporal Joseph S. Bruno, PFC Lyle S. Dunable and Sergeant Donald C. Leek, to finish arming the F4F. Suddenly, an F4F, flown by 2nd Lieutenant Eddie Andrews, careened, its port (left) wing hitting the ground. It came directly at Curlee's fighter. "Hit the deck!", someone screamed. The two Wildcats came together in a sickening crash! The force of the impact spun the charging Grumman completely around and back in the direction from which it came.

Hardly thinking, Betchik charged forward as fast as he could. His one thought was to get the pilot out of the plane! It was already on fire and at that instant Betchik could see no one but the pilot. He was slumped forward in the cockpit, limp. As Betchik climbed up on the wing, he could see blood gushing from the pilot's forehead and down onto his

2nd Lieutenant Roger Haberman stands next to a destroyed F4F-4, No.74. The aircraft was hit during the previous night's shelling of Henderson Field, 13-14 October 1942. (Tom Mann)

VMF-121's Chief Metalsmith, Sergeant Frank Mayer served with the Army's 6th Field Artillery unit at Fort Hoyle, Maryland during his US Army hitch in 1940. Mayer turned down a commission in the Army to join the Marines after Pearl Harbor. Here, as a Corporal, Mayer issues commands to his gun crew. (U.S. Army via Frank J. Mayer)

face and shoulder. He opened the canopy enclosure as far as he could and reached in and turned off the ignition. By now the forward section of the plane was aflame. Tongues of fire were shooting out around the cowling and leaping backward toward the cockpit. Betchik paid no heed to the flames. His mind was set on removing the pilot from the F4F. He now recognized "Andy" Andrews and began tearing at the partially opened canopy with his bare hands but the canopy was jammed! Betchik now yelled for help and another Marine climbed up on the other

Corporal Joseph Bruno, VMF-121 armorer, was seriously injured 18 October 1942 when a F4F went out of control on take off and crashed into the Wildcat he was working on. He died of his injuries, 23 October. "A dear friend," recalled Tony Betchik. (Bruno Family via Tony Betchik)

Staff Sergeant James A. Feliton, Naval Aviation Pilot (NAP) at right, with the natives that brought him back to Henderson Field on 22 October 1942. He had been shot down on 19 October. (Tom Mann)

side of the F4F to help. The canopy still would not budge! They both shouted for more help. Others were standing by just watching the event, apparently too dumbfounded to move. Finally those able to move did, and together they managed to tear the canopy off the burning plane.

Betchik and Dunable then tried to lift Andrews out of the plane but could not. Betchik then swung himself astride the cockpit, reached down and grabbed Andrews as tightly as he could. He then was able to lift him out of the cockpit using all the strength he had. Betchik's knees began to shake from the strain and excitement. Now another problem

Lieutenant Colonel Harold W. Bauer, Commanding Officer of VMF-212, was killed in action on 14 November 1942, while leading a flight of VMF-121 pilots against the Japanese. Bauer was highly respected and well liked by all VMF-121 personnel. Colonel Bauer was known as "Indian Joe" and had earned the Medal of Honor for an action in which he shot down four Val dive bombers. (Tom Mann)

Four of the VF-71 pilots that flew with VMF-121 on Special Temporary Aviation Duty (STAD) during the rough days of October and November 1942. (From Left) Lieutenant (JG) Millard C. Thrash, Lieutenant Carl C. Rooney, Ensign Norman V. Brown and (kneeling) Roland H. Kenton. The missing member of the little group, Lieutenant (JG) Harold N. Reese, was absent when the picture was taken. (Tom Mann)

arose. The pilot's seat belt was hung-up. Betchik then handed his knife to someone and yelled, "Cut the son-of-a-bitch off!" By this time the heat was so intense that it singed the hair of Betchik's head and beard. The flames were almost on them.

Finally the seat belt was cut and Andrews was lifted out of his F4F. Betchik swung back down to the starboard (right) wing and grasped Andrews to him. The right side of Andrew's head was resting on Betchik's shoulder. He felt the pilot's blood flowing onto him. The two Marines, Betchik and Dunable, gently carried the inert Andrews to a waiting jeep, whos driver was screaming at them to hurry - only adding to the turmoil.

As they moved toward the Jeep, Betchik held the brunt of Andrews weight to him with his arms grasped firmly under the pilot's armpits, cushioning the left side of Andrew's head on his left arm.

Someone tried to reach through the basketed arms that held the pilot's lower torso, grasping at the .45 automatic Andrews had in the holster strapped to his right thigh. "I'll be damned " muttered Betchik, as he noticed someone trying to untie the leather laces which encircled the pilot's lower thigh. The former prizefighting Marine looked into the eyes of the man trying to take Andrew's pistol and yelled, "You son-of-a-bitch! What do you think you're doin!" "Hell, he won't need it any-more," came the haughty reply. "He's not even dead yet," Betchik

A damaged F4F-4 awaiting repair on Henderson Field. If an aircraft was judged to be beyond repair, it became a source of spare parts for other fighters. Parts were always a problem in the forward areas. (USMC)

A line-up of VMF-121 flyers at Fighter One during November of 1942. (From Left) Major "Duke" Davis, Commanding Officer, 2nd Lieutenants Roy M. A. Ruddell, Roger A. Haberman, William P. Marontate, Cecil J. Doyle, Thomas W. Furlow, Captain Joe Foss and 2nd Lieutenant Arthur N. Nehf. (Tom Mann)

A squadron ground crewman works on an F4F Wildcat in VMF-121's open air repair shop on Guadalcanal during 1942. (USMC via Tony Betchik)

shouted back, "You touch that again and I'll kick your lousy face in!" The unthinking Marine immediately let go of the holster.

The Wildcat was burning fiercely by now and it was difficult to discern the full extent of the wreckage through the smoke and flame. Tenderly, Andrews was set into the Jeep where another Marine held him upright. Betchik and Dunable let go of Andrews just as the Jeep lurched forward, throwing both Marines to the ground. They got back on their feet and went back to the wrecked planes, which, by this time, were a virtual inferno.

"Anyone else in there?", Betchik shouted. No one answered. Corporal Curlee answered "no!" but he was still dazed and groggy from the accident. He had been thrown at least ten feet by the impact.

"Bruno is out," Leek yelled and everyone present thought that all personnel were OK. The fires were, by now, setting off the ammunition in the F4F's machine guns. Bullets were flying in all directions. Everyone in the area hit the deck. Gradually the fire died down. Then the fight-

er's gas tanks blew-up violently, throwing airplane parts over a radius of about fifty feet. Everyone, by this time, had cleared the area in anticipation of such an event. Eventually the flames and heat subsided. The pile of wreckage now emitted just a little wisp of smoke and flame.

Betchik hopped aboard a truck that was headed toward the ready tent at the Southwest corner of Fighter One. It was here that he saw Andrews and overheard the examining doctor tell a corpsman that, "He'll be OK."

After cleaning up and putting on fresh clothes, he began thinking of the event he had just been through. Just then, another tumult arose, people were shouting and a motor was screaming as an ambulance raced out to the wreckage. Betchik rushed across the runway following the ambulance.

Corporal Bruno had been under the wreckage, but had managed to crawl out on his own after some time had elapsed. Blood ran from a badly lacerated lip and two torn shoulders. He was badly burned, espe-

A Grumman TBF-1 Avenger in flight over the Guadalcanal area during 1942. VMF-121 escorted many TBFs on bombing missions during their combat tour on Guadalcanal. (A.J. Bibee)

Aviatorium Number 1 at Noumea (radio call White Poppy) during December of 1942. This was one of two officer's rest camps established on New Caledonia. VMF-121 pilots rested here in December of 1942. (Tom Mann)

cially his legs. "Give me some morphine and a shot of brandy, he said. "I'll be OK." The corpsmen quickly got him onto a stretcher and pulled out for the hospital.

Andrews had impacted the Wildcat's instrument panel when the fighters collided. He received severe injuries to his skull and face. Bruno had been under the wings of the stationary F4F, buttoning-up the access panels that housed the .50 caliber machine guns. Joe Bruno was apparently knocked unconscious to the ground where the wreckage built-up

"To the victor..." A Guadalcanal Marine and the spoils of his war. a captured rifle, flag and other Japanese personal gear. Squadron ground crews and pilots alike often traded for these items, since they had little chance to actually acquire such "spoils." (USMC via George Burianic)

VMF-121 pilots enjoying a period of rest at Noumea, during December of 1942. (From Left) Art Nehf, Tom Furlow, 2nd Lieutenant Donald C. Owen (in headgear), Joe Foss (seated), 2nd Lieutenant Oscar C. Bate, Jr., Roger Haberman (with pipe) and Bill Marontate, standing on right. As usual, Bill Marontate can't tell a story without using typical pilot hand gestures. (USMC via Tony Betchik)

above and on him. On coming partially to his senses, he tore himself through the rubble, freeing himself. Unfortunately, Lieutenant Andrews died later the next day and Joseph Bruno died of his injuries on 23 October.

The Marines in the jungle were once again up against murderous attacks. The Japanese had landed more troops on the island and their main thrust was always toward Henderson Field.

By 20 October, the Japanese were in their best position to retake the airfield. The Marines, and by this time, the Army, were dug in and ready for the attack they knew would be coming. Earlier, on 13 October, the Army's 164th Infantry Regiment had come ashore to bolster the Marine positions on the island. They also brought the new M-1 Garrand rifle with them and it promptly became a high priority item with the Marine Corps rifle squads. The Marines had landed with the old bolt action Springfield 1903 rifle. They liked the '03 for it's accuracy and dependability but the new M-1 had more firepower with it's eight round clip and semi-automatic action (one round whenever the trigger was pulled.)

The Japanese move toward the airfield began on 20 October, when probing attacks were made against our positions. The enemy, attacked

Captain Joe Foss relaxing at Noumea's Aviatorium #1 during December of 1942. His beard became something of a trade mark. (USMC via Tony Betchik)

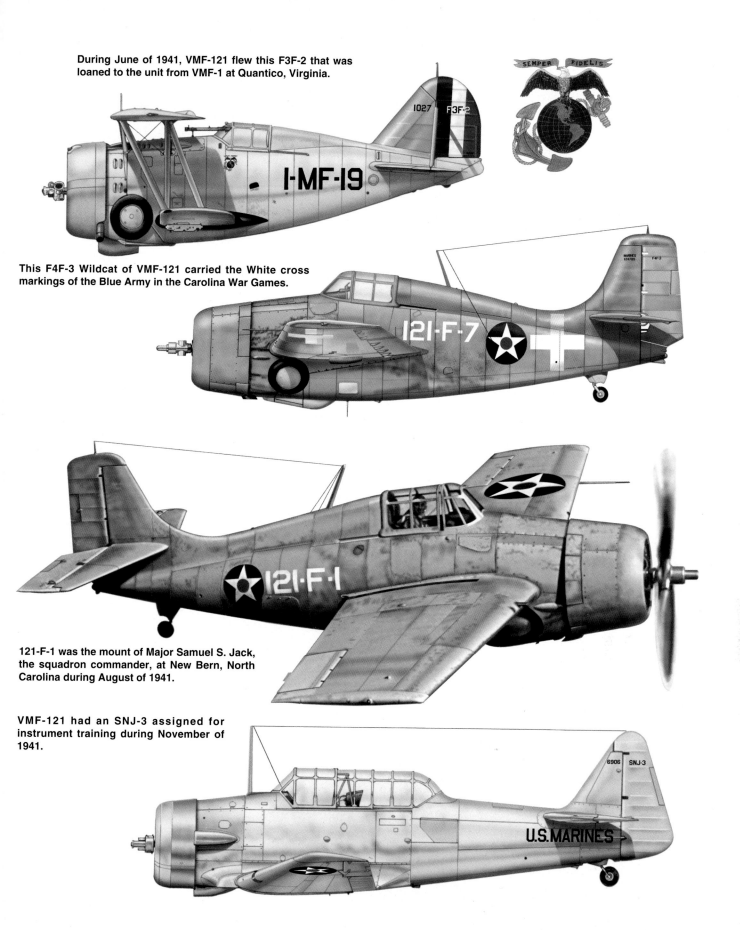

During June of 1941, VMF-121 flew this F3F-2 that was loaned to the unit from VMF-1 at Quantico, Virginia.

This F4F-3 Wildcat of VMF-121 carried the White cross markings of the Blue Army in the Carolina War Games.

121-F-1 was the mount of Major Samuel S. Jack, the squadron commander, at New Bern, North Carolina during August of 1941.

VMF-121 had an SNJ-3 assigned for instrument training during November of 1941.

A TBF of VMSB-131 on Henderson Field during November of 1942. This squadron was the first Marine Torpedo Bomber unit and was often escorted by the Wildcats of VMF-121. (USMC)

with both tanks and infantry, but were beaten back. On 23 October, they tried again.

The Marines along the Matanikau River beachhead came under heavy fire from Japanese artillery and mortars. Tanks once again came into the action but were repulsed. Marine artillery wrecked havoc on the Japanese infantry. The Marines pressed home their counterattack and the enemy retreated, leaving hundreds of casualties behind. The Japanese coastal attack had also been a failure but another day was coming.

The squadron put seven flights into the air on 23 October, beginning at 0515. The most productive flight was the 1100 scramble which saw "Duke" Davis leading thirteen of his own pilots along with ten from VMF-212 and five from VF-71 to intercept yet another flight of Japanese bombers and fighters headed towards Henderson Field.

Davis bagged a Zero, Joe Foss took down four Zeros, Tom Mann scored against a Betty, Greg Loesch and Roger Haberman combined to shot down a Zero (each getting half credit) along with each pilot scoring an individual victory of their own in the fight. Cecil Doyle brought two fighters down with 2nd Lieutenant Roy M.A. Ruddell accounting for another Zero. Bill Marontate got one "smoker" but could not confirm it as destroyed. VMF-212 shot down ten enemy aircraft with VF-71's five pilots, scoring one confirmed Betty bomber and two "smokers."

The early morning hours of 26 October found Lieutenant Colonel

Joe Foss and his Tour One veterans returned to Henderson Field on 1 January 1943. Their arrival back on Guadalcanal was a welcome addition to the "new" VMF-121 that had come aboard during late-December 1942. Lieutenant Colonel Sam Jack, Fighter Commander, Marine Air Group-11, thought the arrival of Foss and "crew", could not have been timed better. (USMC via Tony Betchik)

Lieutenant Colonel Samuel S. Jack, Commanding Officer of MAG-11 during December of 1942. Jack had been the first Commander of VMF-121 during June of 1941. (USMC via Tony Betchik)

Herman H. Hanneken's 2nd Battalion, 7th Marines, under attack by General Masao Maruyama's troops. Hanneken's men had moved west on 23 October to plug a hole in the line along the Matanikau River. The Japanese were trying to advance on Henderson Field but the Marines were just as determined to stop them.

The attack had began at 0200 in the pouring rain and darkness. One of the major thrusts came against an assembled line of heavy and light machine guns commanded by Platoon Sergeant Mitchell Paige. There was fierce hand-to-hand fighting with most of Paige's men either killed or wounded. Sergeant Paige had his machine gun destroyed by Japanese fire. He then ran from one position to the next, firing into the enemy and at the same time looking for surviving Marines. He continued to do this until daybreak. He then came upon an unmanned machine gun position about to be taken over by the Japanese. Paige quickly grabbed the still hot weapon and cradled it in his arms. He then led the Marine defenders down the ridge while firing his machine gun into the enemy. At that point, the Japanese attack broke and the battle was over. Henderson Field remained ours.

The actions of that last week of October resulted in huge Japanese loses. All the men on the island were heroic in their actions. Mitchell Paige and John Basilone were awarded the Medal of Honor for their efforts. Sergeant Paige would later be commissioned in the field as a 2nd Lieutenant on 19 December 1942.

By 26 October it had become evident that the Japanese effort to destroy U.S. Naval and Army Aviation on Guadalcanal had run it's course. October had been a "nightmarish" month for the veterans. That final week of the month had found 121's pilots still making their daily flights. Some were very productive, some merely routine. On 25 October, Joe Foss brought down five Zeros on the 0940 flight. On the

34

Major General Ralph J. Mitchell, Director of Marine Corps Aviation on Guadalcanal during the fighting in 1942. (USMC via George Burianic)

it as he could. Foss eventually had to ditch his plane in the water. After a near death experience in trying to swim clear of his plane, he finally reached the surface and began a hard struggle to reach the island.

His fight to reach the shore took four or five hours. By now it was dark and Foss had just about used up all his strength. He spotted a light in the distance and heard the splashing of oars in the water. Rescue was not too far away. After a few anxious moments, he heard the familiar sound of English being spoken and he knew all was well.

Foss was brought to the island of Malaita and there the missionaries provided a safe haven for the downed flier. Within a few hours Foss would be picked up by a PBY Catalina and be back on Guadalcanal. Captain Foss was back in the air by 10 November for a 1430 flight to familiarize new pilots with the Solomon Islands. He had been gone for three days.

November would see it's share of fighting on Guadalcanal. Marines and Army troops were still fighting off attacking Japanese troops all along the line. The Marines went on the offensive during that first week of November, attacking across the Matanikau River toward Point Cruz. Several days of intense fighting ensued and by 3 November, the Marines halted their advance. The objective, however, was very nearly secured. This attack was put on hold while priorities were shifted eastward toward the Koli Point area. It was here that fresh Japanese troops had been landed and they were starting to make life difficult for the Marines of Hanneken's 2nd Battalion, 7th Marines. Again a fierce battle took place. A few days later the Japanese commander broke off the battle and moved inland. During this move, the Japanese ran headlong into a strong force of Lieutenant Colonel Evans F. Carlson's Marine Raider

Brigadier General Louis E. Wood, Commander Allied Air on Guadalcanal until December of 1942. (USMC via George Burianic)

1310 flight, the Skipper, Major "Duke" Davis shot down a Zero and a Betty. Cecil Doyle scored against a Zero, 2nd Lieutenant Wallace Wethe shot down one Zero on the 1100 flight. Joe Narr brought down two Zeros and a bomber on his first flight of the day. One of the squadron's pilots was shot down that day but he parachuted to safety and the next day 2nd Lieutenant Oscar M. Bate was back and ready to fly again.

On both 26 and 27 October, the Japanese mounted flights against Henderson Field but turned back before getting to the island.

The remainder of October found the squadron taking to the air, but making few contacts with the enemy. Four Japanese dive bombers were accounted for on 30 October and so the month came to an end. On the 31st there were five flights, the most exciting being the 0730 flight made by Tom Mann, John Schuler, Tom Furlow and Bill Marontate. They took off to strafe an area that was supposed to be a Japanese airfield. They completed their mission but failed to see any enemy aircraft. All returned safely.

On 7 November, the squadron almost lost their Executive Officer when Joe Foss experienced engine problems brought on by a rear seat gunner's good luck. Foss' F4F took several hits from a floatplane's rear-ward firing machine gun. This resulted in his engine loosing power and, at the same time, he lost contact with his squadron. On top of everything, his radio would not operate after the engagement. More grief kept coming his way in the form of rain and it was not long before Foss had to put his F4F down, if not on the island he had spotted, then as close to

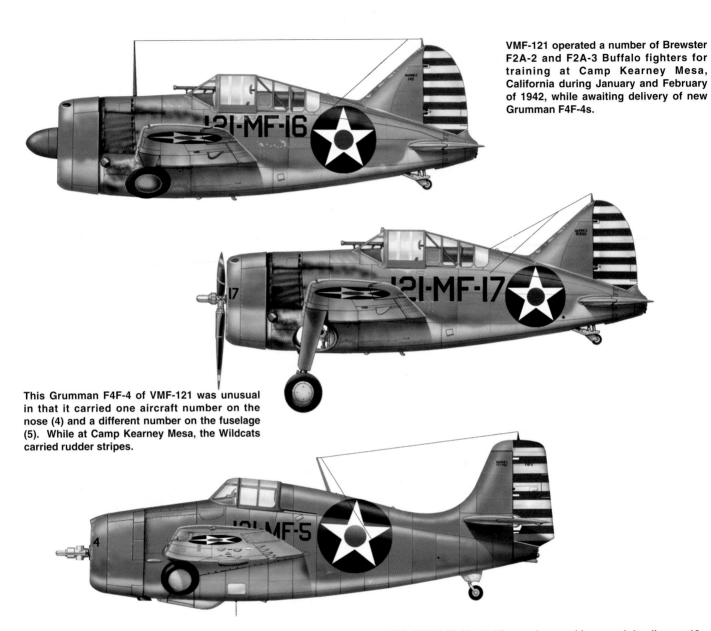

VMF-121 operated a number of Brewster F2A-2 and F2A-3 Buffalo fighters for training at Camp Kearney Mesa, California during January and February of 1942, while awaiting delivery of new Grumman F4F-4s.

This Grumman F4F-4 of VMF-121 was unusual in that it carried one aircraft number on the nose (4) and a different number on the fuselage (5). While at Camp Kearney Mesa, the Wildcats carried rudder stripes.

This F4F-4 (BuNo 5043) was damaged in a crash landing on 13 April 1942. It was later repaired and put back into service.

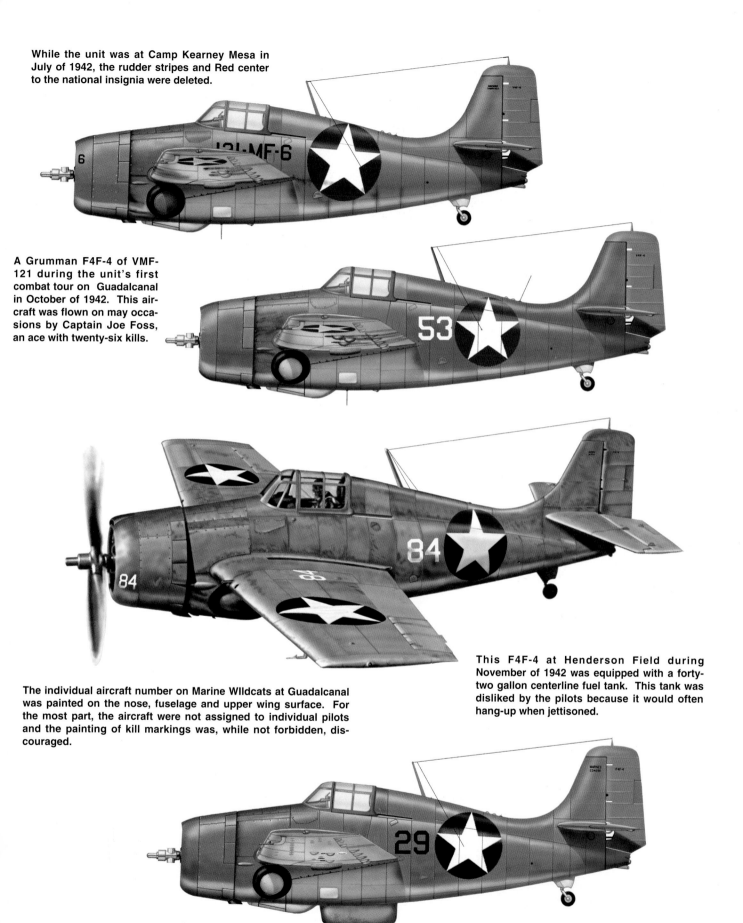

While the unit was at Camp Kearney Mesa in July of 1942, the rudder stripes and Red center to the national insignia were deleted.

A Grumman F4F-4 of VMF-121 during the unit's first combat tour on Guadalcanal in October of 1942. This aircraft was flown on may occasions by Captain Joe Foss, an ace with twenty-six kills.

The individual aircraft number on Marine Wildcats at Guadalcanal was painted on the nose, fuselage and upper wing surface. For the most part, the aircraft were not assigned to individual pilots and the painting of kill markings was, while not forbidden, discouraged.

This F4F-4 at Henderson Field during November of 1942 was equipped with a forty-two gallon centerline fuel tank. This tank was disliked by the pilots because it would often hang-up when jettisoned.

Brigadier General (later Major General) Roy S. Geiger, Commanding Officer of the 1st Marine Air Wing and all aviation units on Guadalcanal. Geiger won Navy Cross in France in 1918 as Commanding Officer of Squadron 7. (USMC via George Burianic)

Battalion. During the days that followed, the 2nd Raider Battalion engaged the enemy in a series of fire fights that saw them engage small groups of Japanese as well as the enemy main force. When it was over, the Japanese had lost nearly 500 men. The 2nd Raiders lost sixteen Marines killed and eighteen wounded.

By 12 November, the Japanese converged on Guadalcanal in yet another massive attempt to take the island from the Marines and soldiers. This action, which began at about 0124 on the morning of 13 November, would be known as the Battle of Guadalcanal. Capital ships

Marine SBD-3 over Guadalcanal, 1942. VMF-121 often accompanied the Douglas dive-bomber crews on their missions against the Japanese. (USMC)

on both sides battled against each other throughout the night. When the sea battle was over, we had lost four of our destroyers with three being damaged. The heavy cruiser USS SAN FRANCISCO (CA-38), was heavily damaged as was the USS ATLANTA (CL-51). Later that day, the ATLANTA would slip beneath the waves, unable to reverse the damage inflicted by the Japanese. The USS PORTLAND (CA-33) also took a beating that night but survived.

The biggest loss of that battle occurred during the morning hours of 13 November, when the Japanese submarine, I-26, torpedoed the USS JUNEAU (CL-52). The loss of ship with some 700 men killed, was especially tragic when it was learned that five members of one family went down with the ship - the five Sullivan brothers. The USS HELENA (CL-50) sustained only minor damage during the engagement.

In the meantime, the squadron was busy flying it's patrols over the area and coming up empty on many of these occasions. The 0915 flight on 11 November proved highly productive for the men of VMF-121.

Major Davis, Greg Loesch, 2nd Lieutenants Samuel B. Folsom, Robert F. Simpson, Donald C. Owen, Joe Narr, Frank H. Presley, David K. Allen, Tom Mann, Roy M.A. Ruddell and Wallace G. Wethe along with Major William R. Campbell of VMO-151, 1st Lieutenant John P. Sigman of VMF-212 and one pilot from VMF-112, scrambled to intercept the enemy flight of Zeros and dive bombers. Contact was made and the fight was on. Greg Loesch shot down one dive bomber, Dave Allen and Frank Presley each brought down a Zero and Sam Folsom received a probable for a dive bomber. "Duke" Davis received a cut on his face when a 20MM shell crashed through the Wildcat's canopy and instrument panel. He returned to Henderson Field and landed safely. Dave Allen

When VMF-121 enlisted men took their rest in Auckland, New Zealand during 1943, they were housed in these little eight man huts. They found them comfortable enough considering the living conditions they had come from on Guadalcanal. The little buildings had eight sleeping racks and a small kerosene heater. (Tony Betchik)

was shot down and parachuted safely to a landing off Lunga Point. He was picked up by a Navy landing craft and was returned to the field fit for duty. The three pilots from VMO-251, VMF-212 and VMF-112, each accounted for a Zero.

VMF-121's Tom Mann was forced to land in the water off Tulagi Island. His story is one of great interest and is told here in his own words, courtesy of his widow, Mrs. Audrey Mann.

"By 11 November I had shot down three bombers and two Zeros. We scrambled that day to intercept a formation of Aichi 99 dive bombers on their way to attack the resupply ships anchored off Guadalcanal. Fortunately, the coastwatcher's alert gave us enough time to take off and climb to 20,000 feet before the Jap planes arrived.

I spotted a flight of twelve dive bombers at approximately 12,000 feet, starting their run on the ships. The dive bombers were on an east course in a rough "V" right echelon. Approximately one-half of the flight had started their dive runs by the time I was in firing position. The remaining six or seven planes started their runs when I began firing short bursts. I opened fire on the last plane in the the echelon in about a 30 degree diving tail shot. The plane smoked and flamed, then fell off to the right. I continued up the echelon and shot down the lead plane in the remaining echelon, continued my roll left and down, and picked up a third Val in it S dive run.

I opened fire at about 1,000 to 1,500 feet and 500 yards distance. The dive bomber smoked and streamed fire. Its bomb either dropped as my bullets hit the aircraft or was released by the pilot. I stayed right on the bomber's tail and fired another burst at about 300 feet. The bomb landed short of a destroyer escort, just as the plane crashed to the northside of it. I don't remember the ship's AA, although they had to be firing away like blazes!

As I pulled out of that dive, I saw a dive bomber at water level, heading north after completing its run. I closed in on his tail. The plane

VMF-121 pilot, 2nd Lieutenant Joseph L. Narr, at Noumea, during September of 1942. Narr was declared Missing In Action (MIA) on 11 November 1942. (Tom Mann)

Captain Joe Foss talks it over with fellow Marines during his post-Guadalcanal war bond tour. (USMC via Tony Betchik)

fish-tailed as the tried to give his rear-seat gunner some shots. I fired a short burst at a distance of about 100 yards. The plane exploded in mid-air about four or five miles north of our ships.

I noticed a fifth bomber heading north after its run, about seven and a half miles directly in front of me. Our speed difference was not very great, and closing with this plane was slower than in my previous encounters that day. As I closed into firing range, I noticed that he was really hugging the deck. His propeller was leaving a prop wash on the ocean. I pulled up to 50-100 feet to get a descending shot and prevent my splash in the water as I tried to shoot him down. Then I noticed another bomber in a shallow right turn a few yards to my left. My flight path was directly in line with his, so I made a flip-turn right. His bullets hit my aircraft that same instant.

My plane was hit in the oil cooler (left wing) and the left side of the cockpit, and I received shrapnel in the left hand, arm and leg. The hits in my cockpit had damaged the throttle and it was now useless. I had really goofed by concentrating on one plane. I have rehashed that flight many times and wonder what would have happened if I had turned into the Japanese plane, rather than away from him. My instinct was to put some armor behind me, because he definitely had me boresighted. I'll never know.

The action had taken place about five miles north and east of Savo Island. I headed south towards home, but the engine quit mid-way between Savo and Tulagi Islands, and I was forced to make a normal,

Captain Joe Foss tours the Grumman factory during early-1943 as part of a War Bond tour. The gentleman pointing to F4F-4's propeller is Leroy R. Grumman, president of Grumman. To the left of Foss is Leon A. "Jake" Swirbul, Grumman's Production Chief. (Grumman)

Although flown by other pilots, aircraft number six was most often flown by 2nd Lieutenant Thomas Mann and it carried his kills under the cockpit.

During the unit's second tour on Guadalcanal in January of 1943, the individual aircraft numbers were for the most part in White.

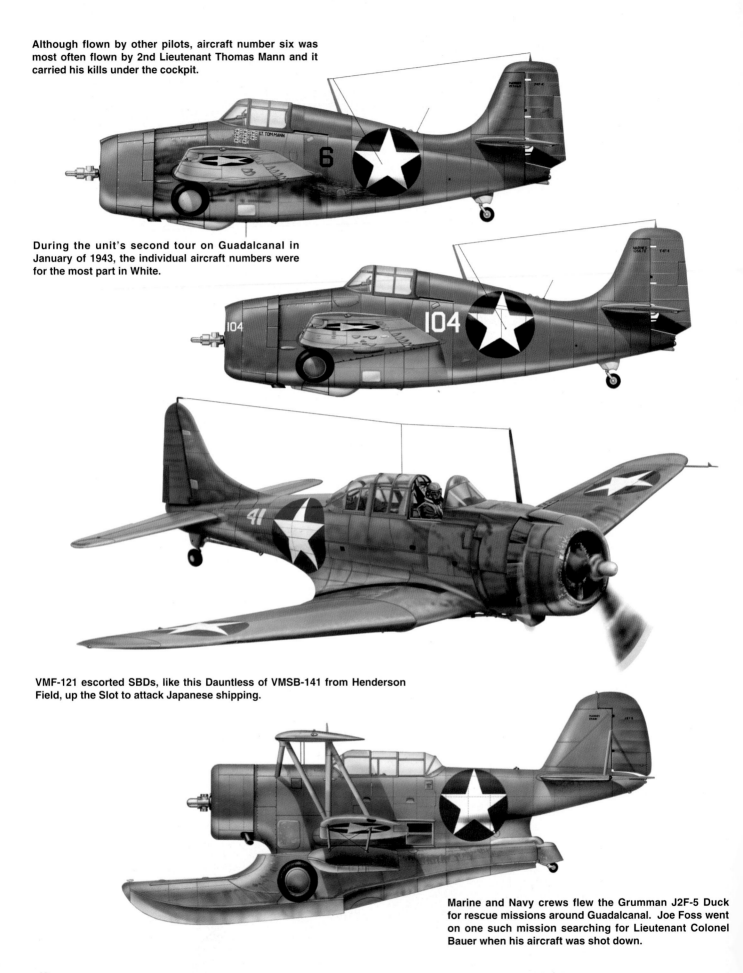

VMF-121 escorted SBDs, like this Dauntless of VMSB-141 from Henderson Field, up the Slot to attack Japanese shipping.

Marine and Navy crews flew the Grumman J2F-5 Duck for rescue missions around Guadalcanal. Joe Foss went on one such mission searching for Lieutenant Colonel Bauer when his aircraft was shot down.

This Wildcat was used by VMF-121 pilots to maintain
proficiency while they were on Western Samoa during
March of 1943.

A Bell P-400 Airacobra of the 67th Fighter Squadron, USAAF on
Guadalcanal during August of 1942. These fighters often flew
alongside the Wildcats of VMF-121.

This ex-VF-17 F4U-1 Corsair was passed to VMF-121 at Mojave,
California for training during November of 1943.

Besides Birdcage F4U-1s, VMF-121 also received a number
of F4U-1As which had a higher, improved canopy.

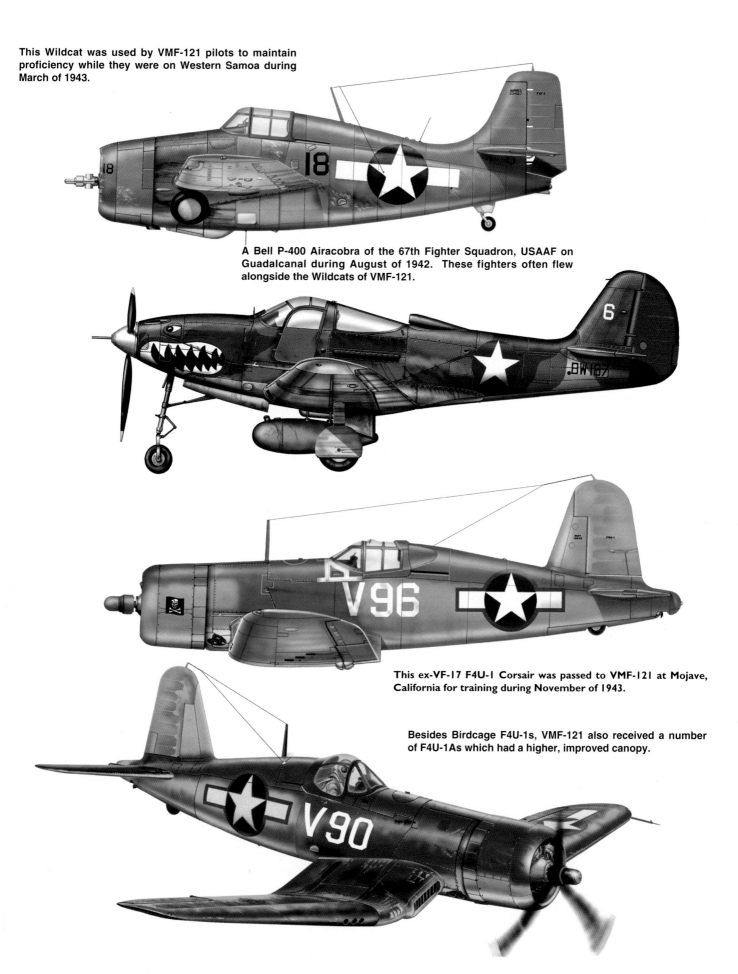

dead-stick landing in the ocean. It must have knocked me out. I came too with water in the cockpit, although the plane was not yet completely submerged. We had no shoulder straps and the impact had thrown me forward. My mouth had hit the gunsight and I had lost five lower teeth and loosened two upper front teeth. I got out of the cockpit and then could not inflate my lifeboat. We had been told that there might be Japs on Savo Island, so I began swimming toward Tulagi in my Mae West.

I swam from approximately 0930 until dusk, when I reached one of the small northern islands of the Tulagi group. The island was only about 200 or 300 yards across with a few coconut trees.

I was lying partially out of the water on the beach when two Melanesian came up and said, "Me watch. Me see." The natives took me in a small dugout canoe to a larger island, the northernmost in the Tulagi group. One of them had been a houseboy for a missionary and spoke broken English and we could converse to a degree.

I remained on the larger island for seven days and my wounds were treated under the supervision of the chief's wife. The treatment consisted of leaves and roots from the jungle that were boiled in water and placed on my wounds with leaves from the solution. I also rinsed out my mouth with the stuff. It tasted awful, but it must have been effective, because there was no sign of infection upon my return. I had two small boys (ages five and seven) who were with me twenty-four hours a day. I couldn't move without them trying to help. The natives were sincere Christians and all members of the village, which consist-

Major "Duke" Davis was awarded the Distinguished Flying Cross, at Faleola, Western Samoa, during March of 1943. (Tom Mann)

Captain Frank Thomas of VMF-112 (left) and Captain Tom Mann of VMF-121 relaxing at Faleola during 1943. (Tom Mann Collection)

ed of eighteen living huts and a central hut, attended a prayer service each evening at dusk. Compared with our lack of of good food on Guadalcanal, the natives' fruits, baked fish and meats were like gourmet foods, even without my teeth.

On 18 November, I was returned to Tulagi in a large dugout canoe with twenty-two natives rowing in sequence waves. The entire trip of approximately forty-five miles was made in about eight hours without a stop. The natives chanted or sang religious songs throughout the entire trip. I returned to Guadalcanal wearing a Jap dungaree uniform that the natives gave me in exchange for my flight suit. They told me that the uniform was from one of three Japs they had killed on their island. The doctors removed six to eight pieces of shrapnel up to one-half inch in size from my left hand, arm and leg. I later received the Navy Cross for the period 25 September through 12 November, 1942, for my actions in shooting down nine enemy aircraft and assisting in two other kills. The action of 11 November had been rough. "

12 November brought VMF-121's tally up another twelve aircraft, two Zeros and ten Betty bombers. The next day, 13 November, the squadron added two Zeros to its score when 1st Lieutenant Otto H. Brueggeman and 2nd Lieutenant Donald C. Owen went out at 0630 along with VMO-251's Major Bill Campbell, 2nd Lieutenant Robert M. Livingston and Herbert A. Peters and VMF-212's John Sigman to intercept a flight of Japanese planes headed for Henderson Field.

11 November 1942 marked a very sad day for the squadron. Master Technical Sergeant Joe Palko lost his life. Joe had crashed his Wildcat near or on Tulagi. The official reports are not precise as to the exact location, however, it was reported that he was found dead in the cockpit, shot through the throat.

Major "Duke" Davis (in jeep) and Tom Mann talk over old times at Faleola, Western Somoa. (Tom Mann)

Awards Ceremony at Faleola, West Somoa on 31 May 1943. (From Left) Tom Mann (Navy Cross), Sam Folsom (Distinguished Flying Cross) and Art Nehf (Distinguished Flying Cross). (Tom Mann)

Joe Palko was regarded as a great guy and morale builder by those in the squadron. Bud Stuckey recalls Joe coming back from an earlier mission with the bullet-proof (thick plate glass) windshield shattered by a direct hit. He told Palko he had nothing to worry about for that was the bullet with his name on it. But, unfortunately, it did not turn out that way.

Stuckey relates that Tom Mann attended Palko's funeral. To quote Tom Mann, "The action of November 11th had been rough." It was, of course, the day that Joe Palko lost his life. He had been on a 1030 scramble along with Joe Foss and Tom Furlow. Roger Haberman received a bullet wound to his right knee and was evacuated to Espiritu Santos on 13 November. Also listed as missing that day were 2nd Lieutenants Bob Simpson, Joe Narr and Roy Ruddell.

On the night of 13th/14th November, the Japanese again sent in their cruisers to bombard the Marines at Henderson Field. The fighter strips also caught their share of steel in this attack. The attack did not last very long, thanks in no small way to a couple of gutsy motor torpedo boats that made a few runs on the Japanese cruisers. Few planes were hit during the shelling and any damage caused to the fighter strips was quickly repaired.

Every plane that could fly from Henderson Field was put into the air to fly against the enemy transports. Cruisers and destroyers were also not

A propeller marked the grave of 1st Lieutenant David K. "Deke" Allen on Samoa. Allen was killed in training accident while at Faleola during 1943. (Tom Mann)

The VMF-121 flight echelon at Faleola. (From Left) Standing, Captains Wally Wethe, Tom Mann, Lowell D. Grow, Art Nehf. Kneeling, 1st Lieutenant David "Deke" Allen and Captain Donald G. Owen. (Tom Mann)

spared in the all-out attack. It was a great piece of work, one that the Marine and Navy airmen had been looking forward to for a long time.

The last engagement in the Guadalcanal area took place on the night of 14/15 November when the battleships USS WASHINGTON (BB-56) and USS SOUTH DAKOTA (BB-57) dueled with the Japanese battleship KIRISHIMA. When it was over, the U. S. Navy had won the day. The KIRISHIMA had to be scuttled.

14 November turned out to be a day of sadness for all the Marines of Henderson Field. At 1600, Lieutenant Colonel Harold Bauer, VMF-212's flight director, led a flight of VMF-121 veterans, Joe Foss, Greg Loesch, Tom Furlow and 2nd Lieutenant Lowell D. Grow. They were to escort a group of SBDs assigned to attack enemy ships in the area. A fight between this little group and the Japanese fighters protecting the ships soon developed when the Zeros came down on the Marines as they were strafing the enemies transports. During this fight Colonel Bauer was shot down and had to ditch in the channel with his crippled F4F-4. He was last seen by Joe Foss swimming out of a large oil slick spreading out in the water. Foss was unable to drop his life raft to the Colonel so he radioed back to Guadalcanal that Bauer was down, then he headed back to Henderson Field where he jumped into a Grumman Duck piloted by Captain Joe Renner. They wanted desperately to fly back to where Bauer was last seen, pluck him out of the ocean and bring him back to safety. By the time they arrived over the area where Bauer was last seen, it was too dark for any kind of effective search. The next morning Foss took out a flight of six VMF-121 pilots, along with one flyer from VMF-122. The 0520 flight failed to find Bauer but did manage to shoot down two Japanese floatplanes that happened into the area. The search for Colonel Bauer proved negative, Indian Joe Bauer was never seen again.

During the week of 15 November, the U.S. Navy's VF-10 turned over fifteen of their F4F-4s to VMF-121 as Fighting Ten prepared to rejoin their ship, USS ENTERPRISE (CV-6), which was anchored in the harbor at Noumea in the New Hebrides Islands. The "Big E" was undergoing repairs and routine maintenance and would soon begin taking on replacement aircraft.

By this time, mid-November, Guadalcanal was not yet totally secure by any means. There were still thosands of Japanese troops on the island and they were prepared to keep on fighting. The problem, however, for the Japanese was their inability to resupply their troops. Our side had no difficulties in that area. Our lines of resupply were wide open and as the year wound down, fresh troops and tons of material began pouring into the island. New squadrons started replacing those that had been fighting since October. Things were changing on Guadalcanal and while the war weary 1st Marine Division was pulling out, plans were being formulated to stage an offensive to rid the island

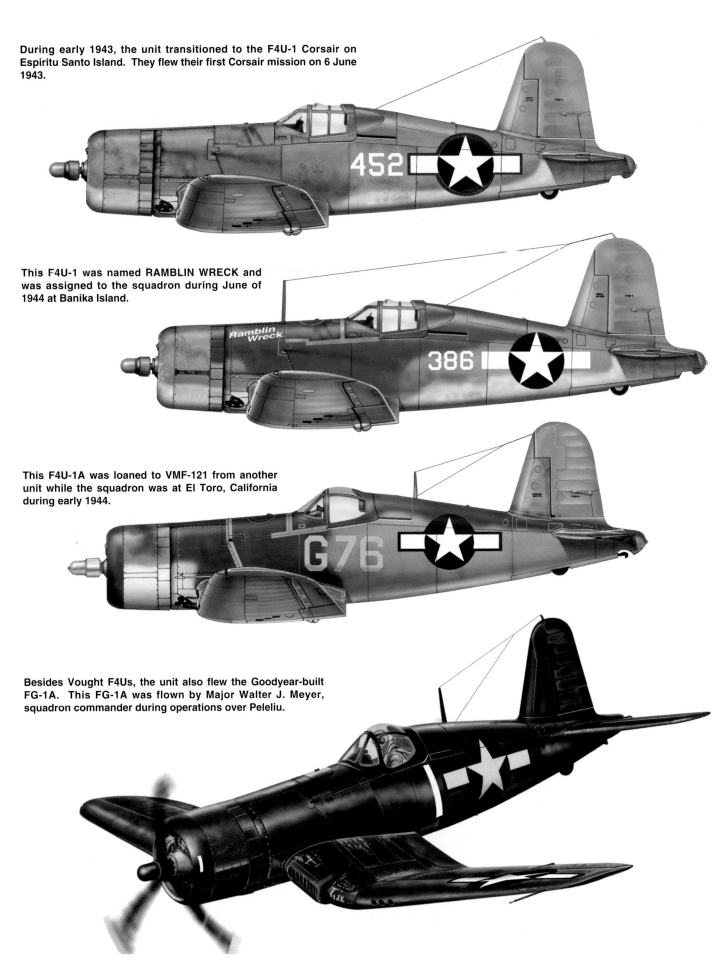

During early 1943, the unit transitioned to the F4U-1 Corsair on Espiritu Santo Island. They flew their first Corsair mission on 6 June 1943.

This F4U-1 was named RAMBLIN WRECK and was assigned to the squadron during June of 1944 at Banika Island.

This F4U-1A was loaned to VMF-121 from another unit while the squadron was at El Toro, California during early 1944.

Besides Vought F4Us, the unit also flew the Goodyear-built FG-1A. This FG-1A was flown by Major Walter J. Meyer, squadron commander during operations over Peleliu.

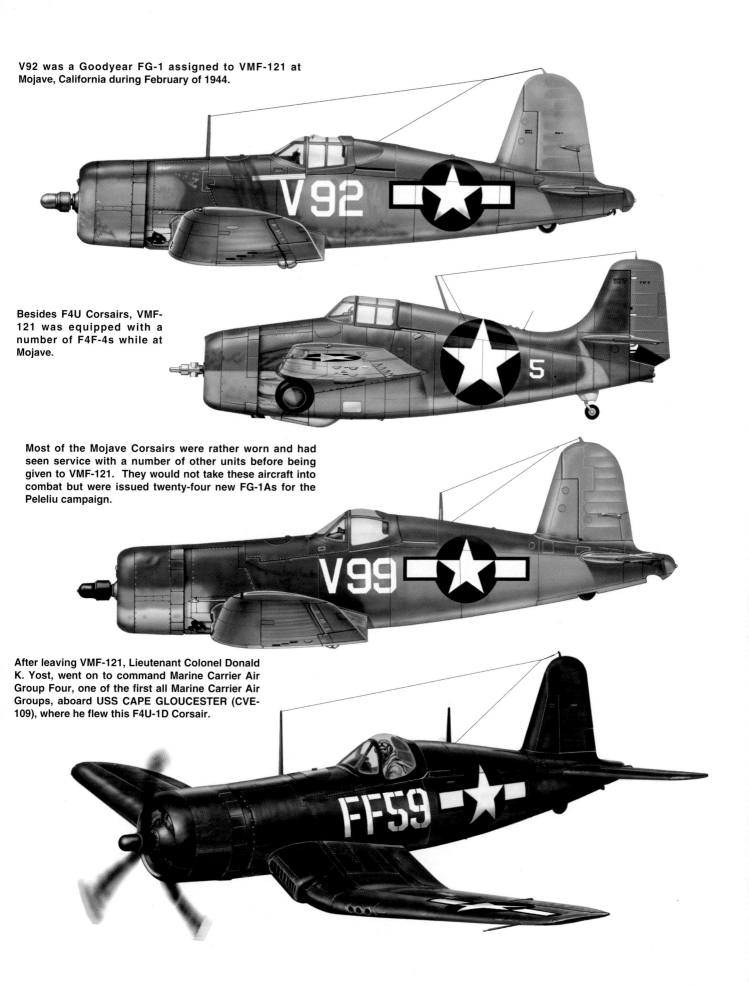

V92 was a Goodyear FG-1 assigned to VMF-121 at Mojave, California during February of 1944.

Besides F4U Corsairs, VMF-121 was equipped with a number of F4F-4s while at Mojave.

Most of the Mojave Corsairs were rather worn and had seen service with a number of other units before being given to VMF-121. They would not take these aircraft into combat but were issued twenty-four new FG-1As for the Peleliu campaign.

After leaving VMF-121, Lieutenant Colonel Donald K. Yost, went on to command Marine Carrier Air Group Four, one of the first all Marine Carrier Air Groups, aboard USS CAPE GLOUCESTER (CVE-109), where he flew this F4U-1D Corsair.

of all enemy troops.

Combined units of Marine and Army troops had to fight some tough skirmishes during the final phase of the Guadalcanal operation. The Japanese did not intend to hand over the island to us without a fight. By the first week of February 1943, Guadalcanal would finally be declared "secure."

Things were also winding down for the men of VMF-121 toward year's end. Most of the pilots that came to Guadalcanal with the squadron were relieved by 19 November. The last recorded kill of that original group occurred on 15 November when Joe Foss and 2nd Lieutenant Oscar M. Bate, Jr. each brought down floatplanes during the futile Bauer search/rescue flight. For the time being, the weary veterans of VMF-121 would have a chance to recuperate in beautiful Sydney, Australia and Noumea.

Starting in mid-December, most fighter operations shifted to Fighter Two, about two miles NW of Fighter One. The old strip proved just too vulnerable to flooding whenever it rained. New names as well as the old familiar ones would now populate VMF-121's roster. On 23 December 1942, a group of pilots, former VMF-111 and 211 members, landed on Henderson Field in an R4D transport and found out they would be the "new" VMF-121. Major Donald K. Yost, being the senior pilot of this group, was made Commanding Officer of the squadron. The formal date of his command status was 1 January 1943, but the very afternoon of their arrival, Yost led two sections of F4Fs on a strafing mission against the Japanese airfield on the island of New Georgia at Munda Point.

The mission was successful, with seven enemy aircraft being destroyed on the ground. The flight ran into opposition in the air as they made for home. The group managed to shoot down four Zero fighters.

Marine Gunner Edward L. Zielinski was one of the enlisted Naval Aiviation Pilots who joined VMF-121 for the squadron's second tour on Guadalcanal during 1943. (USMC)

1st Lieutenant William M. Lundin, came to the squadron during VMF-121's second tour on Guadalcanal, during 1943. (Bill Lundin via Steve Blake)

Yost brought down two, with 1st Lieutenant Irwin W. Carter and Marine Gunner Benjamin B. Wisner shooting down one each. Two pilots were reported lost during the flight. Captain David C. Andre eventually made it back to the squadron on New Years Day, while Wisner crashed on Munda and was killed. Not a very pleasant introduction to the local status quo. The squadron's second tour was off and running.

On Christmas Eve, Yost again led a flight of four F4Fs, himself included, on an SBD escort mission to Munda. The 121 pilots were accompanied by nine Army P-39s and four P-38s of the 12th Fighter Squadron, who acted as high cover during the mission. What occurred turned out to be one very busy day at the office.

Yosts' F4Fs followed the SBD's through their dive at the same time managing to engage and shoot down four Zeros already in the air over Munda. On the runway below some twenty additional fighters were lined up waiting to take off. Ten Zeros made it into the air while ten more were destroyed as they sat on the ground.

Major Yost shot down four of the Zeros, with his wingman, 1st Lieutenant Kenneth J. Kirk, Jr., of VM0-251, taking out three others. 1st Lieutenant Joseph E. Cannon got two and Marine Gunner Edward L. Zielinski got his first Zero. The Army's 12th FS accounted for another four Zeros.

VMF-121 flew two more missions against Munda before year's end. On one of these missions, 121's Captain J. Hunter Reinburg led eight F4Fs and four Army P-39s on what was to be an escort flight for fifteeen SBD dive bombers. Reinburg's flight reached the rendezvous point,

VMF-211 pilots at Palmyra Island during 1942. Many of these men became the second tour roster of VMF-121 in December of 1942. (From Left, some names not complete) Top row; Foeller, Max Read, Perry Shuman, Radford West, Henry Ellis, Captain Francis E. Pierce, Herbert Long, Allen. Knelling: John Moran, Marine Gunner Edward L. Zielinski Naval Air Pilot, William M. Lundin, Charles Somers, John Noble, Eisele, and Andre. (USMC)

Savo Island, and began circling the atoll while waiting for the SBDs to materialize. This went on for twenty minutes and still no SBDs. Reinburg was growing impatient as were the other pilots.

Someone wanted to return to Henderson Field, but Reinburg wanted to make the Munda run. The latter mission prevailed. The F4Fs of Reinburg's flight were headed for Munda. The day was ideal, New Georgia was covered with clouds but the area around the island was fairly clear.

On approaching the island, Reinburg searched for a hole in the clouds. Eventually he found one and could see the airfield. Captain Reinburg headed immediately down toward the airstrip and the two Zeros that were about to take off. At least nine enemy aircraft were destroyed on the runway. Gun emplacements also came under fire from the F4Fs. The action was so fast and furious and there were so many targets of opportunity, that the Marines ran out of ammunition before they realized it.

The VMF-121 flight made it back to Henderson Field after being followed part of the way by a couple of Zeros. Being out of ammo and low on gas, Reinburg opted to turn on the Japanese planes and the rest of the flight did likewise. This caused one of the Zeros' to panic and he maneuvered too violently, causing him to drag his wing in the water and crash.

One Marine of Reinburg's flight became separated from the group and managed to knock down three Japanese floatplanes. By then he was well west of Munda and getting farther away from home. As he had

been experiencing engine trouble, he elected to head for Henderson Field. He made it back safely.

Joe Foss and a small group of veteran VMF-121 pilots returned to Henderson Field on 1 January 1943. Lieutenant Colonel Sam Jack, Commanding Officer of Marine Air Group 11 and the original skipper of VMF-121, welcomed Foss and his pilots back to Guadalcanal. Their combat experience would be called upon to help get the newer pilots into shape and perhaps save a life or two.

Their first missions involved making strafing runs on Japanese cargo ships. There were few opportunities for those in Foss' group to score any aerial victories at that particular time. That situation would be short lived.

On 5 January, the little group flew cover for some of our ships engaged in shelling Munda. Naturally, these ships came under attack by a flight of Japanese dive bombers. They were immediately set upon by 2nd Lieutenant Jack B. Gilford, Greg Loesch, Bill Marontate, Frank Presley and Bill Freeman. Foss was not on this flight.

Captain Loesch and Bill Marontate downed two of the attacking Vals, while Gilford, Presley and Freeman got one each. On the way back they were jumped by Zeros, but fought them off with a series of threatening moves as they were low on ammo and did not need the grief of what could have been a situation weighted in favor of the Japanese pilots, fully loaded and ready for bear.

Another full day came up for the squadron on 11 January. They would escort a flight of twelve SBDs up the Slot to intercept and destroy some ten enemy destroyers.

On the way, the squadrons were jumped by fourteen Zeros. VMF-121 had twelve F4Fs on this mission. This made up three sections. Hunter Rienburg led one of the sections, 1st Lieutenant Herbert H. Long and VMO-251's Major William R. Campbell led the other two. Momentary failure to maintain radio discipline by an SBD crewman, caused a communication problem early on when the Zeros were first spotted.

An overall Light Gray F4F-3 Wildcat of VMF-121 during its training period at New Bern, North Carolina in the Fall of 1941. (USMC via William A. Riley)

Captain Joe Foss outside his tent on Guadalcanal during the squadron's second combat tour. It was during this tour that Captain Foss scored his twenty-sixth kill, becoming the first American pilot to better Eddie Rickenbacker's First World War record of twenty-five kills. (Bill Lundin via Steve Blake)

2nd Lieutenant Bertel R. "Ras" Rasmussen poses with one of the squadron's F4F-4s on Guadalcanal. The cartoon character, rare on Marine aircraft, was one of Al Capp's creations from the Little Abner strip. (Bill Lundin via Steve Blake)

2nd Lieutenant Harold E. "Fateye" Gardner in the cockpit of a F4F-4 of VMF-121 on Guadalcanal during 1943. The aircraft was not Gardner's personal fighter and the three kill markings were not his. (Bill Lundin via Steve Blake)

Eventually VMF-121 got the frequency back and not too soon. Some of the F4F pilots acted out of natural instinct and began to defend the SBDs. Just then, the order came through for them to get back and stay with the bombers. A few of the F4Fs were out of position and this made the whole flight vunerable to the attacking Zeros. Lieutenant Long's flight went to the aid of the two trailing F4Fs. This depleted the rest of the flight but was a move that Long had to make. One of the F4Fs, flown by Joe Cannon was hit during the melee and crashed into the sea.

During all this, the Japanese let the SBDs complete their mission. They were intent on getting the fighters. By this time the squadron had formed a tight Lufbery circle in order to protect each other's tails. As the Japanese kept bringing the attack to the F4Fs. They would dive, firing all the way, then zoom back up to higher altitude for another go-around. It was then that Ed Zielinski joined in the circle, going in the opposite direction. This gave the squadron one firing plane against the Zeros and caused them to disengage and return to Munda. Zielinski's action brought down two Zeros and actually enabled the flight to make it back to Henderson Field. Ed Zielinski's F4F took many hits during the fight and he was chased by a lone Zero while he was headed back to Guadalcanal. His guns would not fire due to an electrical fire which had necessitated his disconnecting the system. The Zero pilot "played" with him by flying around him and frustrating the Marine who could not fire his guns. Finally the Zero pilot went into a roll and flew off in the direction of Munda.

Six VMF-121 pilots scored on this mission, bringing down a total of ten Japanese planes. Joe Cannon was the only squadron fatality. Long and 1st Lieutenant Elton Mueller received wounds to the face and legs respectively. Although painful, their wounds did not keep them down for long.

A few of the F4F's were equipped with a forty-two gallon centerline belly tank that had been tested earlier by VF-3 at NAS Kaneohe Bay, Hawaii. The pilots of VMF-121 disliked the tank as it would, more often than not, fail to release when the pilot wanted to get rid of it. Joe

1st Lieutenant Elton Mueller was one of the pilots assigned to the unit for VMF-121's second combat tour. (Ray Toliver via Steve Blake)

VMF-121 aircrews on Guadalcanal on 1 January 1943, just before the unit ended its time on the island. (From Left some names not complete) top row: Lieutenant Savage (USN) itelligence officer, Eldon H. "Duke" Railsback, Bob Baesler, Major Donald K. Yost - Commanding Officer, Ken Frazier, Youell L. "Joe" Crum, Harry J. "Rocky" Coleman, Robert L. "Pete" Petersen, Perry L. Shuman, J. Hunter Reinburg, Harold A. "Tony" Eisele, Sweethelm, Irwin W. Carter, Jack B. Gilford, Robert E. "Rosie" Daigh. Middle row: Frank D. Williams, Jr., unkn, "Doc" Little, (USN) - Flight Surgeon, Virgil G. Ray, Philip R. White, Alexander M. "Sandy" Hearn, Roy T. Spurlock, (VMO-251), Joe H. "Pete" McGlothlin, Jr., (VMO-251), Master Sergeant William J. "Bill" Kopas -NAP, John R. McMahon. Knelling: Harold E. "Fateye" Gardner, Bertel R. "Ras" Rasmussen, Francis E. "Effie" Pierce, Joseph F. Cannon, Lieutenant Colonel Samuel S. Jack, Commander, Guadalcanal Fighter Command, (original VMF-121 Commander, 1941), Warren E. Fisher, Charles P. "Pat" Weiland, (VM0-251), Elton "Shorty" Mueller, Joseph F. Moravec, Jack Foeller, William M. Lundin. (USMC via Steve Blake)

Cannon's F4F had this tank and when last seen, the belly tank on his F4F was on fire. Many of the squadron's F4Fs were equipped with fifty-eight gallon underwing tanks which did not seem to cause the problems associated with the belly tank.

The squadron was now "short" on Guadalcanal. By the 15 January, VMF-121 had just thirteen days left at Henderson Field. 15 January would proved to be the second most productive day for the squadron, the first was 25 October 1942, when the unit racked-up seventeen victories. The 15th also saw Joe Foss score his twenty-sixth kill, breaking the First World War tally of Captain Eddie Rickenbacker's American record of twenty-five victories held since 1918.

The squadron, though short on tour time, still worked hard to do their best in keeping the Japanese away from Henderson Field. During their last days on the island they were often assigned to escort SBDs on their bombing runs against Japanese ships. That duty always seemed to bring them into contact with Japanese aircraft and that helped keep the enemy away from the island. 15 January was one such mission.

The squadron was in the air shortly before daylight and soon joined-up with the SBDs that were on their way to hit the Tokyo Express as they made their way back up The Slot after one of their many nightly visits to resupply their troops on the island.

Leading three flights from the squadron were Hunter Reinburg, Herb Long and 1st Lieutenant Glen A. Loban of VMO-251. While the SBD pilots were busy at their trade, VMF-121 was very busy at theirs. Soon the sky was full of fighters, twelve F4F-4s and at least twenty of the enemy. Reinburg took on the lead plane and hit him repeatedly in the engine area. To him it looked like the fighter had been put out of commission but he could not be absolutely certain since he had lost sight of him when the two planes passed each other at great speed. He then engaged another fighter, this time Reinburg had no doubt of the outcome. Captain Reinburg's score that day was one confirmed and three probables. Others in the squadron had their hands full too. 1st

Captain J. Hunter Reinburg, VMF-121, on Guadalcanal during early 1943. Captain Reinburg scored the last kill for the unit during its second combat tour on Guadalcanal. (Ray Toliver via Steve Blake)

Second tour VMF-121 pilots on Guadalcanal, pose in front of a F4F-4 during early 1943. (From Left) Captain John P. McMahon, Tech Sergeant William J. Kopas, NAP, Bill Lundin and 1st Lieutentant Henry M. Bourgeois. (Bill Lundin via Steve Blake)

Lieutenant William M. Lundin found a Zero in his gunsight and before he knew it, the enemy fighter was on the way down, a victim of Lundin's guns.

The action continued on with Lundin's luck going south after he took a hit while protecting fellow Marine Captain Jack R. Moore of VMO-251. While nursing his F4F's wounds, Lundin was attacked by another Zero. His guns would not fire due to the earlier hits on his F4F, so all he could do was maneuver around this lone Zero and hope for the best. Finally the Japanese pilot left the scene apparently out of ammunition after scoring only one hit on Lundin's plane.

The fight now over, Lundin headed toward Henderson Field. As luck would have it, his Wildcat's engine gave out and he had to ditch between Savo Island and Cape Esperance. After some twenty-eight hours in the water, punctuated by a shark attack and strafing by an enemy plane, he was picked up by a boat and returned to Guadalcanal two days later.

Jack Moore also had to make a water landing and spent four days in his life raft before he hit land. He was back at Henderson Field by the end of the month.

VMF-121 had accounted for nine Japanese planes during that early flight. Captain Francis E. Pierce Jr. got three, Herb Long shot down two, Elton Mueller shot down two and Hunter Reinburg and Bill Lundin got one each. It had been a busy morning for Reinburg's flight and the day was not over yet.

Joe Foss would score his final victory of his Guadalcanal tour on the afternoon of 15 January 1943. His flight left Henderson Field on an SBD escort mission that was sent out to attack Japanese warships north of Guadalcanal. Two divisions went up, Foss led one and Bill Marontate the other. It did not take long for the action to start. The flight soon spotted the two Japanese ships and they were simultaneously jumped by a group of Japanese fighters. Three F4Fs peeled-off to meet the incoming fighters. Meanwhile, a second group of Zeros were milling about and these took all of Foss' attention. Sure enough Foss was soon involved in a fight. By this time several Zeros had been downed by the quick work of Bill Marontate's flight. Marontate, however, himself fell victim to what was believed to have been a mid-air collision between his F4F and a Zero fighter. Joe Foss had observed an F4F falling seaward, minus its left wing but had no way of knowing it was his friend Bill Marontate.

Oscar Bate was being chased by a few Zeros as he headed toward Foss. As Foss was positioning himself to help Bate, he was soon presented with a target directly in front of him, his reaction was immediate... scratch one more Zero. Another fighter came within range and met the same fate. Bate again became Foss' concern as another Zero, on Bate's tail, was about to do the young Lieutenant some harm. Just as the Zero got off his first few shots, Foss fired across his cowling. This got his attention and he turned toward Foss. This brought about a head-on attack, plane to plane. Both pilots missed during that first pass. On the second go-around Foss scored when the Zero pilot turned to the right, exposing his cockpit to the veteran flyer. Foss' rounds hit home but seemed to do no damage to the fighter. That proved to be short-lived and soon the Zero began to smoke and flame. The last Foss saw of the fighter, it was diving toward the ocean.

Joe Foss' flight made for home and landed on Henderson Field in the midst of an enemy air attack, however, they all landed safely. Captain

A second tour VMF-121 pilot, Captain F.E. Pierce, in the cockpit of a F4U Corsair after he transferred into VMF-122. (Ray Toliver via Steve Blake)

Foss got three Japanese planes on that flight and became the leading U. S. fighter Ace with twenty-six victories, breaking Captain Eddie Rickenbacker's First World War I record of twenty-five.

The last action for Foss and his pilots came on Monday, 25 January 1943. Scores of Japanese planes were headed toward Henderson Field. It was up to VMF-121 and its brother squadrons to meet the incoming Japanese aircraft and save the field from yet another attempt to render it useless. The Army got in on it too. The 12th Fighter Squadron's P-38s came up to lend a hand. What followed turned out to be a game of cat and mouse. If our fighters were to go headlong into the enemy fighter formations then that would leave the bombers relatively free to hit Henderson Field. Besides the Zeros, the Japanese also had a sizable force of Betty bombers and a squadron of dive bombers.

Time and time again, the Zeros would drop down to engage our F4Fs and each time the F4Fs had moved to avoid their trap. As time went on more and more of our planes were getting airborne and building up our odds in the sky. A few contacts were made, the P-38s shot down at least two of the Japanese fighters. The game continued, finally the Japanese, impressed with the growing strength of our numbers, gave it up and turned around their attack force and headed north for their home bases at Bougainville and Munda. Henderson Field had made it through another day.

Action on the ground was, by 26 January, pretty much on our terms. By 30 January, the only frontline unit advancing on the remaining Japanese troops was the Army's 147th Infantry. The nightly runs by the Japanese to evacuate their troops continued. By 9 February 1943, Guadalcanal was declared secure. No organized Japanese units remained on the island.

The honor of bringing down the last Japanese plane for VMF-121 on this tour would go to Captain Hunter Reinburg. Flying F4F-4, Bureau Number 03549, Reinburg found out his aircraft did not have a radio only minutes before he was to take off. It seems the radio had been removed for maintenance and to replace it would take too much time. Reinburg was not in the mood to wait around. He told the young enlisted man that

Captain Gregory K. Loesch served with VMF-121 on both it's first and second combat tours on Guadalcanal during 1942-43. (Ray Toliver via Steve Blake)

Besides the underfuselage fuel tank, which was widely disliked by VMF-121 personnel, their F4F-4s also carried fifty-eight gallon under-wing fuel tanks, either singles or in pairs. The pilot on the wing is unidentified. (Bill Lundin via Steve Blake)

he would take the plane even though it did not have a radio.

Heading for Savo Island he used standard hand signals to communicate with his wingman Elton Mueller. After signaling to Mueller that his radio was not operating properly, Reinburg then gave the lead to Mueller since he had an operating radio. The flight then proceeded back toward Henderson Field. Mueller had received orders over the radio to do so. This would put them into a good position to attack any approaching enemy bombers. Reinburg did not quite agree, as he wanted a shot at the fighters he had seen earlier on the way back to the Guadalcanal area. Captain Reinburg was not was not at all sure this was the order that Mueller received but it seemed logical to him that that may be have been the case. He then took the lead over from Mueller by way of another set of hand signals and proceeded to dive away and to the right. Just then he spotted a Japanese fighter. Rienburg prepared to attack the Zero and quickly found that this particular pilot knew his trade. The Zero pilot made all the right moves. He just failed to make enough of them. Reinburg got him with an overhead attack and only stopped firing at the Zero as he passed behind him.

The powerful forces brought against Reinburg's body during this fight temporarily caused him to lose effective use of his eyesight, he almost blacked-out. Fortunately he regained his faculties in time to see the Zero burning and headed for a jungle grave.

Next he saw another Zero about 3,000 feet below him coming in the direction of his F4F. He engaged the fighter but could determine if he scored any hits on him, so fast was the action. Not too long after that encounter, Reinburg latched onto another Zero, this time he very definitely saw the enemy plane disappear before his eyes. Victory number two. Reinburg found more Zeros on his personal fighter sweep, but since he was now low on gas, due to running at full throttle, he thought the better part of valor would be to head for Henderson Field and live to fight another day.

Reinburg's exuberance necessitated his performing a victory roll over Henderson Field, a fitting end for VMF-121's Guadalcanal tour. All of the squadron's pilots made it back on 27 January. The Japanese force turned back again, dropping their bombs in the sea.

The next day, 28 January 1943, VMF-121 received orders to evacuate the island. Guadalcanal was now only pages in a history book for the squadron but the personal memories would live on forever in the men that risked everything to keep that hot and humid patch of land in the South Pacific.

The toll: 2,799 Marines wounded, 147 Marine Aviation personnel killed, 127 Marine Aviation personnel wounded, 1,152 Marine officers and enlisted men killed, 446 Navy and Army personnel killed, 1,910 Navy and Army personnel wounded. "I've served my time in hell."

Corsairs

Following the second tour on Guadalcanal, the pilots of VMF-121 found themselves going in many different directions. Some wound-up going to the newly organized VMF-121, some went to Sydney, Australia for a rest and some went to other squadrons. The squadron's enlisted men made their way to Auckland, New Zealand with stops along the way at Efate and Espiritu Santo. They deserved all the good times they were able to handle. "Duke" Davis took over as Commanding Officer of VMF-111.

In the meantime, VMF-121 was being reorganized on Espiritu Santo at Turtle Bay. They were the recipients of a new, more powerful fighter that was to replace their old F4F Wildcats. The squadron began to re-equip with the Vought F4U-1 Corsair fighter on 15 April 1943. The trusty little F4F was now only a memory, the new fighter would carry them through to VJ Day. The first Marine Corps squadron to fly the F4U in combat was VMF-124. They began flying from Henderson Field on 11 February 1943, with Major William E. Gise commanding. VMF-121 personnel began arriving at Henderson Field on the first day of June 1943. Some of her pilots came in by an R4D (C-47 Skytrain) transport while seventeen VMF-121 pilots flew in with their new F4Us.

Included within the squadron were a few combat veterans from VMF-121's second combat tour. The new skipper, Major Raymond L. Vroome, had never fired a shot in anger but he fully understood the value of the experience of some of the younger men in the squadron.

Marine F4U-1 Corsair fighters scramble from a coral airstrip in the Russell Islands area. There was a wide variety of markings applied to the F4Us during this period. (USMC)

Building upon this, he and the other yet to be tested in combat flyers, worked well and hard to bring everyone on line to get the job done.

The squadron's first combat patrol in the F4U took place on Sunday, 6 June 1943. Captain Robert M. Baker, Captain Louis Gordon, 1st Lieutenants R.F. Foxworth and N.A. McCartney flew the "knucklehead" ("Knucklehead" - Banika) patrol in the Russell Islands area. No contacts were made and all returned safely.

The next day the squadron took to the air at 1010 to cover our shipping in the Tulagi area. Ten F4Us made the flight, but once again, no contacts were made but two pilots, Vroome and 1st Lieutenant W. H. Snee, ran out of gas and had to make water landings. They were picked up by OS2U Kingfishers later in the day.

The next day, 8 June, thirteen pilots from the squadron flew to the newly established airbase on Banika Island. The 3rd Marine Raider Battalion had landed there in February, unopposed, and provided a foothold in the Russell Islands. VMF-121 was to spend the night at Banika and fly escort for a combined TBF and SBD mission against the Japanese at Kahili. On 9 June, the mission was called-off and the pilots returned to Henderson Field.

The twelfth day of June finally gave those squadron pilots without combat experience the opportunity to rectify the situation. At 0945 the squadron scrambled eight planes to intercept a flight of Japanese planes

Captain Bruce Porter in the cockpit of his F4U-1 Corsair on Banika Island during 1943. (R. Bruce Porter)

reported near the Russell Islands. Captains E.M. Schmidt, Bruce Porter, Bob Baker, Kenneth M. Ford, R.L.Bryson, T.F. McEvoy, with 1st Lieutenants Philip J. Leeds and William B. Harlan took to the air to meet the incoming Japanese fighter sweep. Shortly after leaving

A SBD Dauntless dive bomber of VMSB-141 parked on Henderson Field, Guadalcanal. VMF-121 continued to escort Marine SBDs and TBF Avengers with their new Corsairs while flying from Henderson Field. (USMC)

Henderson Field, Captain Bryson had to return due to engine trouble. The rest of the group pressed on.

Most of the Japanese planes were encountered between 21,000 and 29,000 feet. Bruce Porter got involved with one of the many Zeros in the air that day. His first shots barely missed their target. The Japanese pilot then had his chance at Porter, but he too missed his prey. Porter again maneuvered into another advantageous position only to have his tracers miss their mark as the Japanese pilot pulled his Zero straight up and out of range. Porter then found himself in the middle of massed confusion, aircraft were everywhere. Suddenly, he had another Zero in his sight. Now he had his man. At about 300 yards, Porter opened fire and the enemy fighter blew up before his eyes. This was his first victory, one he would never forget. As quickly as it had all started, it was over and the individuals involved began heading for Henderson Field.

Phil Leeds, Porter's wingman, got his first kill on this flight and another over Cape Esperance on the northwest tip of Guadalcanal. McEvoy contacted Zeros at 29,000 feet over the Russells, but did not score. Bob Baker made contact over the Russells at 25,000 feet and during this fight, scored a probable out of the six fighters he engaged. Ken Ford found his Zeros at 21,000 feet and shot down two with another as a probable. Harlan landed at Banika, but returned to Henderson Field at 1400. He reported downing one Zero with two as probables. He also reported seeing an F4U Corsair down in the water. This may have been Schmidt, but they never knew for certain and Schmidt was later listed as missing in action.

At about this same time, the code name system adopted in mid-1942

Lieutenant Colonel Donald K. Yost, Commander of Marine Air Group 4, heads his F4U-1D down flight deck of USS CAPE GLOUCESTER (CVE-109) on 7 April 1945. Lieutenant Colonel Yost was a former Commanding Officer of VMF-121 during the squadron's second combat tour on Guadalcanal in December of 1942 and January 1943. (USMC)

Pilots of VMF-121 accounted for many of this type of Japanese fighter during their Second World War combat tours. This Mitsubishi A6M5b Zero, Model 52b, has major damage to its horizontal stabilizer and has started its final plunge toward ocean. (USN)

for identifying Japanese aircraft began to creep into the vernacular of some Marine pilots. This system was devised by Captain Frank T. McCoy, Jr. as a way of simplifying the names of Japanese aircraft. The system used male names for fighters and female names for bombers, ie. Zeke for the Mitsubishi A6M Zero and Betty for the Mitsubishi G4M bomber. In spite of the new identification system, the name Zero from the original Japanese Navy designation, A6M1 Type 0, was still referred to by some Marines for the remainder of the Second World War.

The twelfth of June saw the squadron bring down six enemy aircraft and suffer the lose of one VMF-121 pilot. Japanese air activity was virtually put on hold for the rest of June, 1943. There were two occasions when Japanese aircraft were spotted, on 18 and 20 June, but they left the area before any action could be taken against them. On 16 June, the squadron moved to Banika Island in the Russell Island chain. VMF-121 was the first fighter squadron to be assigned to the airstrip on this island. Banika was code-named Knucklehead and was classified as an advanced base.

On 20 June, Bill Harlan totalled his F4U Corsair while landing at Knucklehead about 1600. He was only slightly injured. On 28 June, the squadron lost 1st Lieutenant William H. Snee, when his F4U spun-in from an altitude of 500 feet just east of the end of the landing strip and about 100 feet from Lona Island, while he was taking off. His F4U exploded when it hit the water.

Progress up the Solomons Islands chain was soon on the move. The plan to take New Georgia was put into action with the main objective being the airfield at Munda. A series of landings took place over a period of fifteen days. One of the major landings took place on 30 June and VMF-121 was one of the squadrons assigned to cover the landings on Rendova and New Georgia.

VMF-121 was in the air at 0545 on the morning of 30 June. Captains Louis Gordon, Jim Poindexter, R.E. Schneider, Warren H. McPherson, Frank Pierce, G. W. Wilcox, Bruce Porter and T. F. McEvoy with 1st Lieutenants Caruth A. Barker, Jr., Bob Foxworth, Henry McCartney, Vernon L. Glascock, R. M. Rhodes, Phil Leeds and Rex L. Linde were on station by 0645. Several of the pilots had difficulties joining up with their sections and returned to Banika. They would fly again later in the day.

Bruce Porter made contact at around 11,000 feet over Rendova while covering the troops. He saw about twenty Zeros, but no bombers. He attacked and shot down one Japanese fighter. He also hit another but could not confirm its demise. His Corsair had been hit and this made it necessary for him to start for home. Phil Leeds had been flying wing on Porter and had also earned his combat pay on this flight. He had chased a persistent Zero off Porter's tail thereby repaying Porter for a similar occurrence that took place between the flyers earlier.

On this flight, Leeds reported seeing Zeros, with round wing tips, painted Dark Green or Black with the Rising Sun wing and fuselage insignia outlined in a very dark color. He also saw a clearing and hut on the highest peak on Pavuvu and thought it was possibly that of a Japanese coastwatcher.

Lieutenant Barker, flying wing on Louis Gordon at 11,000 feet over Rendova, saw four Zeros about 1,000 feet below with several more two or three thousand feet above. They dove on the four Zeros below them. Barker shot down one then saw a Zero shoot Captain Gordon's F4U, causing it to smoke. Gordon was seen flying into a cloud and upon emerging from the cloud, he was seen to bail out of his F4U. Louis Gordon did not make it back.

Captain Perry L. Shuman of VMF-121's second flight, which went out at 0925, contacted six Zeros and shot down two of them before his Corsair's gun jammed. After clearing his guns in a nearby cloud, Shuman returned to the fight and shot down another enemy aircraft. Shuman had been a division leader with the squadron during their second tour flying from Henderson Field in F4F-4s. In the Russells, on the squadron's third combat tour, he was its Executive Officer. He was also the high time flyer on both tours.

Bob Baker took on seven Zeros southeast of Rendova at about 12,000 feet. When it was over he had brought down three of his adversaries. Hank McCartney made contact, hit one Zero, saw it smoke but not crash.

Captain William H. Whitaker, of the second flight, made contact over Rendova at 15,000 feet with eight Zeros. He shot down one. He reported seeing three Zeros with square wing tips, most likely the Mitsubishi A6M3 Model 32s. He reported the aircraft as being painted Light Gray overall and the wing and fuselage insignia was out-lined with a darker color than the Red of the Japanese national insignia. He also saw a dark fuselage band, aft of the aircraft's cockpit, and thought it was probably eighteen to twenty-four inches wide.

Captain Kenneth M. Ford, of 121's second flight, shot down two Zeros before flying into a large bank of clouds. When he came out of the clouds he saw another Zero and quickly shot it down. He also reported seeing an F4U go down in flames.

Captain Harold R. Trenchard made contact at about 9,000 feet. He had lost the use of his radio and did not know the fight was on. While over the water between Rendova and Munda Point, a Zero made a pass at another aircraft, he could not see. The Zero came up directly ahead of his F4U and performed a roll. Trenchard lined him up in his sight, gave him a good burst and the Zero blew up practically in his face. Bill Whitaker's F4U joined-up with him and the two pilots continued the fight. Trenchard saw two F4F-4s from another squadron fighting two Zeros but did not see the out-come. He then found another Zero in his

Four pilots from VMF-121's third combat tour, pose for photos during an awards ceremony at Marine Corps Air Station El Toro, California in November of 1943. (From Left): Captain Kenneth M. Ford, Captain William H. Whitaker, Captain R. Bruce Porter and 1st Lieutenant Rex L. Linde. (R. Bruce Porter)

path and finished him off with a short burst. He then made for home.

At 1355 a third flight went out to cover the Rendova and New Georgia assaults. On this flight, eight VMF-121 pilots, Jim Poindexter, Bob Schneider, Warren McPherson, Vern Glascock, Frank Pierce, George Wilcox, Captain Hardy Hay and 1st Lieutenant R. M. Rhodes took up station over the landings. Shortly after take-off, three of the pilots returned to base due to engine trouble.

McPherson and Glascock, flying at 500 feet, saw a lone Betty bomber about 100 feet off the water. The bomber had just unloaded her bombs at several U.S. warships going through the pass between Rendova and Tetaperi Islands. The two pilots used perfect teamwork, with each one taking up a position on either side of the Betty. They proceeded to make side approaches on the aircraft and while weaving, McPherson fired several hundred rounds causing the bomber to flame and crash into the woods on the southern tip of Rendova.

VMF-121 pilots at "Knucklehead," the advance base- on Banika Island in the Russell Islands chain on 11 May 1943. (From Left) front row: 1st Lieutenant P. J. Leeds, Klas, Captain F.E. Pierce, 1st Lieutenant R.M. Rhodes, 1st Lieutenant W.B. Harlan. 2nd Row: 1st Lieutenant W.H. Snee, Captain E.M. Schmidt, 1st Lieutenant H.A. McCartney, Captain L. Gordon, Captain R.B. Porter, Morace. 3rd Row: Captain T.F. McEvoy, Captain H.R. Trenchard, Captain W.A. Baron, Captain R.M. Baker, Captain G.W. Wilcox, Captain R.E. Schneider, Captain R.L. Bryson. 4th Row: Andre, 1st Lieutenant R-L. Linde, Major R. L. Vroome, Commanding Officer, Captain H. Hay, Captain W.H. Whitaker, Captain P. L. Schuman, Captain K. M. Ford. (R. Bruce Porter)

This F4U-1 Birdcage Corsair (BuNo 02386) named "Ramblin Wreck" was formerly assigned to VMF-121 during the squadron's third combat tour at "Knucklehead." When the squadron was reassigned, the aircraft was left for the next squadron coming on line. The aircraft was still on Espiritu Santo on 8 March 1944. (USMC via Jim Sullivan)

In that same area, Frank Pierce, George Wilcox and Jim Poindexter were all flying together when they came upon a couple of Betty bombers that had just made an attack on our ships in the channel. Pierce and Wilcox made a head-on pass on one of the planes and caused it to flame on its port (left) side between the fuselage and engine. Poindexter had concentrated his fire on the aircraft's tail section. He saw his tracers hit the Betty's tail gunner. He then moved over to the aircraft's port side and continued firing until it crashed into the sea. Captain Pierce reported this Betty was well camouflaged, Dark Brown with a White background. It also made good speed, approximately 200 knots or better.

Captain W.A. Baron, of the 0925 flight, who had been reported missing, was brought in by LST around 2400. He had been flying on Porter when contact was made west of Rendova at about 12,000 feet. They mixed it up with eight to ten Zeros as he continued to fly on Porter. Suddenly, Zeros came up from below plus some from above and all concentrated on him. He received several 20MM in his F4U's wings and fuselage and a 7.7 round cut the line from his receiver to his earphones. Finally a 20MM round hit inside his cockpit and exploded. This threw shrapnel along his right leg from the hip to the ankle while also hitting his radio, causing it to blow up and make a great cloud of smoke. He then rolled over and dove down to 2,000 feet and started back for Banika.

On the way home he ran into a heavy weather front southeast of New Georgia. Weak from loss of blood and blacking out, he turned around and went back a few miles where he had seen a small convoy. He proceeded to locate this group of ships and made a water landing. He was picked up immediately by an LST. There was a Corpsman onboard and he was given life saving aid until he could be returned to Banika.

30 June had been a true Red letter day for the squadron. VMF-121 had accounted for nineteen Japanese aircraft while covering the New Georgia landings. This topped the 25 October 1942 score of seventeen the squadron racked-up during its first tour on Guadalcanal. Overall, the Marine Corps claimed fifty-eight Japanese planes shot down during the engagement of 30 June. The final twenty-one days of 121's third combat tour would see them account for eighteen more enemy aircraft.

The agenda for 2 July 1943 was to patrol the area around Rendova Island. Mechanical problems seemed to descend upon the squadron's F4Us. Bruce Porter's plane experienced landing gear retraction problems on both his 0645 and 1321 flights. Dick Baker's F4U kept overheating. Vern Glascock's engine would not operate properly and Bob Foxworth experienced the same difficulty. The planes that stayed in the air that day managed to find enough action to make up for the ones that had to be left behind.

The 1315 flight made contact east of Rendova at about 10,000 feet. Bob Baker estimated there were about forty Zeros at about 15,000 feet. The Zeros, upon spotting the F4Us, dove on the flight and the fight was on. Baker quickly brought down two Zeros. Perry Shuman heard Baker yell over the radio that the Zeros were attacking from above and he instinctively went into action. The result was two Zeros shot down and one listed as a probable.

Rex Linde found that he was the target of three or four Zeros and dove into a cloud after being hit in the fuselage by a 20MM shell. He then climbed to 20,000 feet where he saw six Army P-38 fighters but could not attract their attention. He then elected to carry-on without them. Linde dove on a flight of twenty to thirty Zeros that were flying at about 5,000 feet and shot down one, then he headed for home.

Harold Trenchard took several 20MM hits and after taking stock of the damage, decided he was most likely not going to make it home. He did manage to make it to North Field in the Russells, landed his almost totalled F4U while feeling lucky to make it back but a little disappointed that he had not fired a shot in anger during his flight.

Hank McCartney shot down one Zero on his flight but he too found himself on the receiving end of Japanese fire. His F4U barely made it back to North Field after being escorted by Bob Baker and Perry Shuman. Ken.Ford and Caruth Barker were reported missing on this flight. Ford made it back, Barker did not. McCartney reported seeing Barker being driven down toward the sea by several Zeros and that Barker disappeared into a cloud and that he never saw him again

Some Japanese bombers did get through to bomb our troops landing on Zanana Point on New Georgia. We suffered fifty-nine killed and seventy-seven wounded.

Dick Rhodes, missing since a 1 July B-24 escort flight to Kahili, came back on 3 July. He had his oil line break over Kahili. He radioed the trouble but was not heard. He then started for home. He flew over the Shortlands to Vella Vayella then over to Kolombangara then over to the north side of New Georgia, just over Vanguna. At this point, his engine was so bad he knew he would not make it home. He circled one native village but saw no one. He then sought out another village and this time spotted several men in canoes. He decided to land in the water next to the natives. When his F4U came to rest, the men in the canoes paddled over to him and helped him out of the cockpit and into one of their boats. Shortly afterward he was on an LST headed for Banika.

1st Lieutenant Robert Dailey, Jr., missing since 30 June, turned up at Banika courtesy of a Navy LST. He had been flying wing on Perry Shuman and shot down one Zero before he took several hits from **VMF-121 trained at Mojave with the Goodyear duplicate of the Vought F4U-1. The FG-1 made up the largest compliment of the squadron's aircraft but they did have a few of the Vought-built Corsairs. This F4U-1 was attached to the VF-17 then, taking part in the shakedown cruise of USS BUNKER HILL (CV-17) during July of 1943. VMF-121 inherited at least one of VF-17s aircraft while at Mojave and flew the aircraft still carrying the old unit's insignia on the cowl. (USN)**

Japanese 7.7 and 20MM shells. One went through his wing and another exploded beneath his F4U's cockpit. Dailey then dove for the sea and hoped he could make it home. Just opposite Viru Harbor, his engine froze. He then decided it was time to leave his stricken F4U. He bailed out at 3,000 feet. When he hit the water he immediately inflated his rubber boat. It was not long thereafter that he was spotted by an LST crewman and taken aboard. He was then taken to Oloano Bay, Vangunu Island while the LST crew unloaded supplies and took on wounded. Within days he was back with VMF-121.

Ken Ford had a similar situation occur when his F4U was hit by 20MM fire and he found his oil line had been cut. He managed to stay in the air for about thee minutes; enough to get over to the west side of Rendova, a little south of the harbor.

He fired his guns to attract attention as he landed in the water. He inflated his rubber boat and was only in the water about an hour when he was picked-up by a Higgins boat crew which took him to Rendova, from which he was flown to Henderson Field in a Navy PBY Catalina. He arrived at Banika, courtesy of a Marine Corps R4D, on 5 July.

On 5 July, the squadron put eight pilots into the air at 0730 to cover our destroyers in Kula Gulf. This mission was successful. By noon, the flight was back at Knucklehead. Warren McPherson, taxiing to his revetment, hit a tree and damaged his F4U's wing. On a later flight, at 1200, Hank McCartney, Harry Trenchard and Perry Shuman, each shot down a Zero. Trenchard also claimed one probable. McCartney took a 20MM hit in his right wing but made it home.

The squadron welcomed a friend from the second tour on 10 July when Don Yost checked-in for a brief stay. He had been Commanding

A F4F-3 Wildcat from Marine Corps Air Station Mojave, California. VMF-121 was reformed at MCAS Mojave in October of 1943. They flew a few F4F's, but concerned themselves mainly with becoming combat ready in their new fighter, the Goodyear FG-1 Corsair. (USMC via George Burianic)

Officer of 121 during its short second tour at Henderson Field. Yost took off at 0630 along with seven other 121 pilots to fly escort on B-25s that were to look for and attack reported Japanese shipping in the area. They never found the B-25s and returned to Banika at 0730. Don Yost would later command Marine Carrier Air Group 4 on the USS CAPE

GLOUCESTER (CVE-109), when it became an all-Marine carrier in 1945. On 5 August 1945, Yost would shoot down his eighth and last Japanese aircraft of the war. His flight on 10 July with 121 would be his one and only on the third tour.

The push to capture the airfield at Munda finally ended in August when Major General Oscar W. Griswold, commanding the Army's XIV Corps, took it with his 43rd, 25th and 37th Infantry Divisions. In November of 1941, VMF-121 had attacked General Griswold's bridgehead at Camden, North Carolina during the Carolina War Games to help win it for the Blue Army.

VMF-121 pose in front of a Goodyear FG-1 at Mojave, California during 1944. (From Left, Kneeling): 1st Lieutenant W. A. Keag, 1st Lieutenant H. C. Hawkins, 1st Lieutenant B. A. Fornonzini, 1st Lieutenant W. A. Bates, Captain P. J. Leeds, 1st Lieutenant V. B. Perry. Standing: 1st Lieutenant G. O. Beal, Major J. W. Poindexter, 1st Lieutenant C. M. Canan, 1st Lieutenant M. E. Spooner, 1st Lieutenant C. P. Libeau, Major Q. B. Nelson, 1st Lieutenant A. M. Kelly, 1st Lieutenant W. F. Brown, Lt(jg) R. M. Kash (Flight Surgeon), Major W. H. Clay, (Executive Officer), Major W. J. Meyer, (Commanding Officer), 1st Lieutenant S. D. Watson, 1st Lieutenant. J. S. Reid, Major R. G. Snowden, Captain H. Hay, 1st Lieutenant J. M. Thompson, 1st Lieutenant G. W. Dodson, 1st Lieutenant R. L. Gillis, 1st Lieutenant W. E. Cooley. Starboard wing: 1st Lieutenant W. R. Hoover, 2ndLt. J. M. Buchman, 2nd Lieutenant J. D. McVay, 1st Lieutenant J. A. Carmena, 1st Lieutenant W.L. Faulkner. Cowl: 1st Lieutenant R. L. Stults and "Slipstream," VMF-121's Mascot. Port wing: Captain R. M. Rhodes, 1st Lieutenant J. E. Deen, 1st Lieutenant S. E. McGinty, 1st Lieutenant W. H. Fisher, 2nd Lieutenant L. D. Jensen. (George Burianic)

The biggest strike of the squadron's third tour took place on 17 July. Besides the four Marine fighter squadrons assigned, VMFs 121, 122, 213 and 221, the Army would supply a P-38 squadron and the Royal New Zealand Air Force would assign a P-40 squadron. The "Kiwis" were to be low cover for the main attack group. The main attack group consisted of eighteen SBDs from VMSB-132, eighteen more from VB-11 and thirty-five glide-bombing TBFs plus the "heavies", seven Army B-24 bombers. The Marine fighters would fly high cover with the P-38s flying over the entire group. VMF-121 joined-up with the TBFs that were headed for Buin and Kahili. The flight had commenced at 0740. The first contact was made at 1115 by Rex Linde, Warren McPherson, Bob Schneider and Bill Whitaker. There were five or six Zeros. During the ensuing fight, Rex Linde nearly came to grief when a Zero, apparently hit by a fellow 121 pilot, almost cut his F4U in half as it fell from the sky in its death plunge toward the sea. Whitaker made a pass on a Zero and scored several hits sending the enemy fighter to a watery grave. Warren McPherson, wheeling around in a tight turn, saw a Zero in his sight and gave him a quick burst, sending him seaward. He also hit another enemy aircraft but did not see him crash.

Vern Glascock made contact at about 14,000 feet over Kahili. He soon found himself pursued by several Zeros. McPherson came to Glascock's aid and chased off the attacking fighters. Within seconds the threat was over. Almost immediately, Glascock saw a Zero making runs on two men in parachutes. He fired on the Japanese fighter and sent it crashing into the water. He then pulled-up and saw another Zero tangling with an F4U. He gave him a burst and brought him down. Glascock pulled his F4U up to about 5,000 feet, when his fighter stalled and went into a spin. He managed to restart his engine just as he found two Zeros coming at him from either side. He then turned on one of the fighters and headed for cloud cover. He then climbed to 12,000 feet and started for home. As he looked back he saw a lone Zero at about 4,000 feet below him and decided to dive on the unsuspecting pilot. Glascock made his pass, firing as he dove. The Zero's right wing fell off and the fighter crashed into the sea. Glascock made it back.

Phil Leeds made contact at 1125 at about 8,000 feet. He saw four Zeros and also saw many other planes taking-off as he approached the island's airfield. His rounds failed to hit their mark but fellow pilot, Bill Whitaker, scored several hits and shot down the Zero. Leeds saw a cruiser hit and sinking.

Bruce Porter would soon score his third kill on this flight. He also received credit for one probable. He made contact at 1125. He saw two Zeros closing with two F4Us. He flew right up into them and started shooting at one of the Japanese fighters. His rounds found their mark and the Zero went into the sea. He then found another Zero and managed to hit him but he would not go down. Porter later reported that this pilot "Gave me a bad time." When it was over, the, Zero got away and Porter observed one F4U go into the water about forty miles west of Vella Lavella and saw bombers hit an oil tanker and cruiser. "Good weather" all the way he reported. The raid was successful that day. The fighters had done their job.

The last victories of the squadron's third tour took place on 18 July 1943. Dick Rhodes and Bob Dailey took the honors by downing one Zero a piece while escorting a flight of Army B-24s to Kahili. It was an early flight, 0730. Dailey made contact at 1050 when he spotted a Zero on Perry Shuman's tail. Dailey was able to give him a shot and he went down. Shuman credits Dailey with saving his life that day. Shuman's F4U developed engine trouble and he had to head for home. Dailey accompanied him and kept two more Zeros off his crippled F4U on the way back to Banika.

Dick Rhodes, at about 8,000 feet, saw an F4F being chased by a Zero near Vella Lavella. Rhodes gave him a burst and saved the F4F pilot. He saw another F4F pilot make a water landing between Kahili and the Shortlands. The pilot got out of the F4F and inflated his raft. He appeared to be OK and Rhodes, low on fuel, had to make for home.

VMF-121 1st Lieutenants Claremce L. Harsher, Stanley D. Watson, Andrew M. Kelly, "Slipstream", and Christopher M. Canan, gather for a "briefing" on the horizontal stabilizer of a FG-1 Corsair (BuNo 13244) at Mojave, California during 1943. (USMC via George Burianic)

Due to his lack of fuel, Rhodes had to land at Segi Point on the southern tip of New Georgia, where we had an emergency airstrip.

VMF-121's remaining days on this tour now numbered three. Patrols were sent up on 19 and 20 July. On the 20 July flight, Perry Shuman, Bob Dailey, Hank McCartney and Bob Foxworth, reported seeing a burning PT Boat about thirty miles south of Kolombangara. One other PT was standing-by while two more were observed heading for Rendova. By 1000 the flight was back at Banika.

The last day of the third tour, 21 July, found VMF-121 flying escort on Army B-25s looking for enemy shipping. The 0700 flight was uneventful. There was some anti-aircraft fire from the Japanese destroyers protecting the transports but it proved ineffective.

There were a couple of patrols later in the day but they went off without incident. Hardy Hay, Frank Pierce, George Wilcox and Harry Trenchard flew cover for a PBY rescue to Enogai Inlet at 1720, that proved routine. After that mission they escorted Army bombers to to Bairoko Harbor. They strafed the Japanese on the west side of the harbor and experienced heavy anti-aircraft fire from Vila but made it back OK.

On 22 July it was over. The squadron gave up its F4U Corsairs to the incoming VMF-214. They then boarded R4Ds and PBYs for the flight to Henderson Field. 23 July was spent winding down and awaiting transportation to Turtle Bay, Espiritu Santo in the New Hebrides, then on to Tontouta on New Caledonia. After a seven day lay-over, the

Major Quintus "B" Nelson and Major James W. Poindexter of VMF-121 hold a discussion alongside the unit's single Vought F4U-1, V-96. The Corsair was previously flown by VF-17 and still has this squadron's insignia on engine cowling. (USMC via George Burianic)

F4U aviation mechanic Private First Class George D. Burianic in the cockpit of V-90, the Corsair he took care of at MCAS Mojave. (George Burianic)

A Vought F4U-1A on touch down at Marine Corps Air Station El Toro, California during a VMF-121 training flight in early 1944. The "G-76" side number was in Orange-yellow. (USMC via R.L. Lawson)

Lieutenant Richard M. Loughery, checked into Mojave.

July was an especially busy month for the squadron. It was decided that VMF-121 would make a cross-country flight to Naval Air Station North Island, San Diego, California to board the USS RUDYERD BAY, CVE-81, for Carrier Qualifications (CarQuals) training. Fifteen of their Corsairs made the flight and were hoisted aboard the little carrier as soon as they had checked in at San Diego.

During this time period, 5 July through 8 July 1944, the squadron carrier qualified twenty-three pilots and they actually had only one good day in which to do it. On the second day of operations, the wind all but died out completely, ending all flight operations for the day. This condition continued on into the next day. It now became apparent that these conditions would remain for the schedule of the squadron's deployment aboard RUDYERD BAY. It was then decided to send those pilots, who had not yet qualified, back to Mojave. They were catapulted off the carrier on 8 July. The carrier qualified pilots rode the ship back to San Diego.

The RUDYERD BAY's Captain, Captain C.S. Smiley, noted that while he thought some of the squadron's Corsairs looked as though they had been gathered together as "sacrifices", he thought that VMF-121's mechanics had done a remarkable job of maintaining their aircraft. He went on to say that his carrier based mechanics would do well to emulate the Marine mechanics. He also felt that the F4U type aircraft was an excellent carrier aircraft. This was due in large extent to the pilots and crewmen of VMF-121. On 10 July 1944, Commander Fleet Air, West Coast, declared VMF-121 Carrier Qualified.

Changes were in the air and the pilots of 121 were getting "itchy" and

VMF-121 mechanic Private First Class Al Arkromos in front of a FG-1 Corsair, V-99, on the ramp at Mojave. (William J. VerMuelen)

were growing impatient with the desert routine.

On 12 July, 1st Lieutenant Richard L. Stults, flying a FG-1A (BuNo 13787), ripped off two feet of his fighter's right wing when he hit a Joshua tree while on an unauthorized strafing run. He was unhurt and brought the damaged FG back without further problems.

On the same day, VMF-121 turned in their twenty-three FG-1As and the lone F4U-1 to MBDAG-44 and prepared for embarkation in the USS KWAJALEIN (CVE-98), bound for Espiritu Santo in the New Hebrides Islands. The squadron's fourth combat tour was now eminent.

The trip took seventeen days during which the squadron attended daily classes in aircraft recognition, navigation, survival, intelligence and the performance and characteristics of Japanese aircraft.

On 4 August 1944, VMF-121 checked-in at Turtle Bay and began setting up for flight operations. They received twenty-four new Goodyear FG-1A Corsairs on 6 August and immediately started combat testing of their new fighters. They were now part of Marine Air Group Eleven (MAG-11).

The squadron now entered upon a concentrated regimen of division tactics. The amount of aircraft involved varied between thirteen and eighteen on any given day.

On 21 August, one of VMF-121's third tour veterans, Captain Phil Leeds, departed the squadron for Headquarters Squadron Marine Air Group Eleven. His combat experience would be missed. During this period of time, the newer pilots in the squadron spent time practicing their dive-bombing runs on a target located on the island of Rabaul.

The invasion of Peleliu was now off the planning boards and would soon become a reality. On 4 September, the squadron began staging for

V-92 serves as a backdrop for VMF-121 mechanics and metalsmiths at Mojave during 1944. (From Left) Top row: Corporal Bill VerMeulen, Sergeant Walter V. Dobosz. Kneeling: Sergeant Robert J. Walsh, Corporal Charles E. Smith, Jr. (William J. VerMeulen)

A VMF-121 pilot, 2nd Lieutenant William H. Fisher, Jr. and his plane captain Sergeant Allen L. Corless in front of V-92, Mojave, California. (William J. VerMeulen)

Private First Class Edward E. Widdick, one of the Corsair mechanics, in front of three of the squadron's FG-1s on the apron at Mojave, during 1943. (William J. VerMeulen)

the Peleliu operation. Thirty of its forty pilots were moved via F4U and R4D from Espiritu Santo to Emirau via Guadalcanal and Bougainville. Twenty-four FG-1As were flown over-water during this transfer. At Emirau, more practice in section and division tactics was carried out. This went on from 5 September to 25 September.

The ground echelon arrived on Peleliu on "D" Day, 15 September 1944, to prepare for the arrival of the flight element. By 20 September, a small camp had been set-up. Many men of the ground echelon served as stretcher bearers, grenade throwers and riflemen with the 1st Marine Division while awaiting the pilots and aircraft of the squadron.

Among the ground echelon of VMF-121 to land on Peleliu was Corporal William J VerMuelen, one of the squadron's metalsmiths. The letters that he wrote to his parents were in the form of a day to day record of what he saw or experienced. He was fortunate enough to have one of his life long friends with him on Peleliu, his name was Bud (PCF Cornelius E. Kiewiet, VMF-121 aircraft armorer). As was typical, VerMuelen downplayed the extremely difficult events so as not to worry his parents any more than they already were. A small slice of what daily life was like for the enlisted Marine, just doing his job, is presented here.

A Vought 0S2U-3 Kingfisher directs naval gunfire during the opening phase of the Palau Islands invasion on 15 September 1944. Some VMF-121 ground crews went ashore during the early phases of the invasion to prepare for the squadron's arrival, approximately one week later. (USN)

A Grumman TBF-1C Avenger became the first combat aircraft to land on the Peleliu airfield when it was forced down after it ran out of fuel on D+4. The port main landing gear leg appears to have sunk in the soft surface off the side of the runway. (USMC)

16 September 1944 (D+1)

"It has been a long time since you heard from me. There are a lot of

Marines ashore on Peleliu during initial landings of 15 September 1944. The VMF-121 ground echelon went ashore as riflemen and fought side by side with Marine infantrymen. (USMC)

things I would like to tell you, but they sill have to wait till I get back to the good ole USA. This island is in the Palau Group and I imagine you have read about it in the newspapers.

Bud and I were separated, but we met again two days ago." (note: VerMuelen and his friend Bud were on different troop ships on the way to Peleliu. A few days after the landing on Peleliu, Vermuelen was on the beach observing a bomb truck coming ashore at low tied. The truck got stuck on the reef and the Japanese began zeroing-in on the stuck vehicle with their mortars. The Beachmaster yelled for someone to run a cable out to the truck to wench him free VerMuelen helped carry out the cable. When he got to the truck he discovered the driver was his friend Bud.

"You ought to see the foxhole we have. We were talking last night how we did just about everything together, we went to church and school, then worked together and now in the same foxhole together. A year and a half ago our big concern was not to be late for a softball game, etc. Don't worry we are both safe and sound."

25 September 1944 (D+10)

"I imagine by the time you get this, Peleliu will be old news but I will never forget this place as long as I live. The Japs fought like mad men, and would not quit. Dad, I know you would have liked to been along, because it was really something to see. Especially the night before the first wave went into the beach. The big battleships, cruisers, and tin cans opened up on the island. I did not think there would be

64

an island left in the morning. Don't worry, Bud and I are both OK."

1 October 1944 (D+16)

" We have been eating C-Rations, but today our cooks used a make shift galley and cooked a warm meal. Boy it was good, canned chicken, biscuits and corn. Until now a bunch of us guys would throw anything we had into a big can and heat it up. We had some fancy mulligan stews."

6 October1944 - (D+21}

"We had our first mail call in quite a while. Both Bud and I received forty-five letters. What a time we had lining them up according to dates."

10 October 1944 (D+25)

"I no longer have the camera, and my fountain pen has a hole in it. All of my stuff is gone." (Note: A shell exploded over VerMeulen's foxhole and destroyed most of what he had with him. All he suffered was a very bad headache. It was at this time that Sergeant Richard C. Millage was severely wounded and died the next day, 3 October.) "I will tell you about it when I get home. Please send me a cheap pen as they are impossible to get out here. An officer in another squadron had a pet pig until the other night. The pig got loose, was going through the brush when a guard thought it was a Jap, fired in the general direction and killed it. The officer who owned the pig was furi-

A F4U-1D belonging to VMF-114 begins its take-off roll on Peleliu's airstrip. VMF-114 flew missions along side VMF-121 from Peleliu as part of Marine Air Group Eleven. The unit was commanded, at that time, by Major Robert F. Stout who had been Special Temporary Aviation Duty (STAD) with VMF-121 during the Guadalcanal campaign. (USMC)

ous, this pig had been with this outfit for two years, they moved him wherever they went, he was a real pet. I don't blame the guard, as I have had guard duty myself and the Japs continue to try and sneak thru the lines."

15 October 1944 (D+30)

"I have been to some odd places for church services, but the one I will never forget is the service held on board ship while the battleships and planes were shelling and bombing just before the first wave moved onto the beach. It just didn't seem real to be singing the same hymns out here just like we used to do in church at home. One huge difference was when we sang hymns like "Abide with Me," etc., the words meant a lot more.

When we stopped at Guadalcanal we picked up some of the First Marines. What a tough looking bunch of guys. They have been out here over twenty-seven months and have been on the 'Canal, Tulagi and Cape Gloucester. I talked to several of them on the way up here. They have been over so long, and seen so much that they don't "give a rip" for anything or anybody. They have all resigned themselves that they will never see the USA again, they are all old men at only 18, 19 or 20 years old."

26 October 1944 (D+40)

"That little pup we had in Espiritu Santo died before we left. When we came here we did not have one dog, now we have three of them. Where they came from I don't know, but a dog is a valuable asset out here and if anybody gets a chance to swipe one from another outfit, they swipe him. A couple of dogs belonged to the Japanese. One of them looks like a Wire Haired Terrier. He will sit up and bow his head when he begs for food. I guess the Japs like to teach dogs tricks too.

You ought to see the barber shop one of the guys set up. He has a

A Marine SB2C-4 Helldiver flys over Yap Island during August of 1945. VMF-121 flew many missions against targets on Yap during their stay on Peleliu. (USMC)

sign that says *121 Clip Joint, Come in Sucker, C.A. Coffee, Prop. The squadron had a barber kit and Coffee decided to cut hair. He does a pretty good job now, but you should have seen some of his first creations.*"

11 November 1944 (D+54)

"*There was a beautiful sunset tonight. We can look out over the ocean from our tent. The sun looks like a ball of fire down here, and you can see it sink in the ocean. This island used to be pretty too, before our Navy and the bombers gave it a going over. Just before the first troops hit the beach the barrage was so terrific it looked like the trees were being mowed down by a big lawn mower.*

I never told you about the party the officers gave us before we left N.H. (New Hebrides). Everybody was feeling good as they had plenty of beer. They threw the officers in the drink, right then we found we had a good bunch of 'Joes' for officers as everyone of them took it, laughed and even helped throw in the rest of the dry ones. When you see a Major in the Marine Corps get tossed into the ocean (and not very gently at that) then you know that everyone has to be feeling good."

25 December 1944 (D+98)

"*Christmas Day on the rock. We had a terrific dinner, fresh turkey, potatoes, etc. Everybody got an orange. I ate mine section by section making it last as long as I could. From now on we are supposed to have more fresh food. We were getting tired of canned hash & stew.*

It won't take much for me to be satisfied on Christmas after this."

12 January 1945 (D+116)

"*Our carpenter Bill Golding (Sergeant William H. Golding) and Ackerman (PFC Percy J. Ackerman, Jr.) with some help have built an open air theater with confiscated lumber. Just to show you how starved these guys are for entertainment, just about the middle of the show every night it will start to pour rain, but nobody makes a move to leave and the show keeps on going. Everybody just sits there and keeps watching the screen as though nothing has happened. If somebody would have told me a year ago that I would sit in the rain to see a show I would have told them they were crazy.*"

29 July 1945 (D+314)

"*We have new pilots, these new guys are pretty good, they put on a show the other day flying over in formation, spelling out 121.*"

10 August 1945 (D+325)

"*I had just started to write this letter when some guy came tearing down between the tents yelling the Japs had quit. Everyone is going nuts. It is now early in the morning, we are all setting around the radio waiting to see if the United States will accept the surrender. Immediately, everybody started talking about going back to civilian life. It does not seem possible. Most of the guys admitted they were scared to go back to civilian life. One kid said, "that means no more garbage details for me. On the other hand, it means I will have to go to work, I think I'll sign over.""*

5 September 1945 (D+351)

"They gave us the word that we will be boarding ship for home three days from now. It don't seem possible that by the time you receive this, we will be on our way."

1 October 1945 (Pearl Harbor)

"Pearl Harbor, we are back in civilization again and you can't imagine how good it is to be back. I had four malted milks, one after another. They give us anything we want."

The fighting on Peleliu turned out to be some of the roughest of the war. Again the main target on the island was its airfield. This particular field was one of the strongest and best equipped in the Japanese Mandates. Capturing this airfield would put U.S. forces within 500 miles of Mindanao in the Philippines.

Peleliu lacked natural water sources and had to depend on rainwater captured in storage tanks. This patch of coral, roughly five miles long and two miles in width at its widest point, would be VMF-121's home for almost a full year.

The landings were made by the First Marine Division. Marines of the 2nd Battalion, 5th Marine Regiment, almost immediately drove eastward at first then turned northward toward the airfield, they would be the first to get a piece of that valuable property.

Before the airfield became ours, two aircraft from VMO-3 landed on the island on a cleared piece of land. They were light, high wing observation types, Consolidated OY-1s. The next day, 20 September, the Marine Observation squadron began operations from the newly captured

Major Walter J. Meyer, Commanding Officer of VMF-121 and on his left, Major Claude H. Welch. Welch would later become Commanding Officer of VMF-121 when Meyer left for the States. (Walter J. Meyer)

Old, reliable Grumman J2F-4. The Duck rescued many pilots in the Pacific during the war. It was in a J2F that Joe Foss and Joe Renner searched in vain for Harold Bauer after he was shot down on 14 November 1942. (USMC)

airfield, thus becoming the first Marine Corps squadron on Peleliu.

On 24 September, VMF(N)-541 started operations on the island with their night fighting Grumman F6F-5Ns, commanded by Lieutenant Colonel Peter D. Lambrecht. VMF-114 and their F4U-1D Corsairs under the command of Captain Robert F. Stout, came in on 26 September. Bob Stout, while a member of VMF-122, had flown with VMF-121 on STAD during the squadron's first combat tour on Guadalcanal. VMF-122, with former 121 member Hunter Reinburg in command, came in on 1 October with their F4U-1D fighters. Five days later, VMTB-134, equipped with their TBF-1s, came in to round out Marine Air Group Eleven's presence on Peleliu.

The fight for Peleliu was every bit as hard as it had been for Tarawa and Saipan. Peleliu was declared secure on 27 September, however, total security would not be established until 27 November 1944.

When VMF-121's flight echelon came aboard the island, they brought twenty-three FG-1A Corsairs with them, with five additional pilots coming to the island in a Curtiss R5C-1 transport.

The first combat air patrol assigned to the squadron occurred on 27 October. The flight, commanded by Captain Hardy Hay, took off at dawn. The four Corsair flight made no contacts and all returned safely to base. Major Meyer's 1600 flight brought the day's activities to an end, again no contacts were made.

Enemy air activity at Peleliu was nowhere near what it had been during the squadron's previous combat tours. Because of this, the squadron would be assigned to barge sweeps and bombing missions up and down the island chain.

The first fire taken by the squadron on this tour came on 30 October. During a barge sweep over Babelthuap Island, 1st Lieutenant Robert L. Gillis' FG was hit in the left tire, right wing, wing root forward of the wing flap and in the rear portion of the cockpit area. Gillis managed to bring his badly damaged Corsair home.

The next day, the squadron experienced its first loss of the Peleliu tour. 1st Lieutenant George O. Beall, the squadron's parachute officer, was part of Major William Clay Jr.'s 1240 flight on a mission to bomb the Japanese airfield on Yap Island. After one of their dives, George Beall did not rejoin the formation. Major Clay circled the area of the Gagil-Tomil Airfield, searching for Beall or any sign of wreckage, but he could not locate him or find any evidence of his fate. The flight returned to base at 1645 and Beall was listed as Missing In Action (MIA).

On 9 November, the squadron experienced a really hair-raising event

On Peleliu, the heat dictates the uniform of the day for at least five of VMF-121's mechanics. (From Left): Private First Class Benjamin P. Van Iderstine, Corporal Robert J. Walsh, Private First Class Arthur D. Mauplin, Private First Class Charles E. Smith, Private First Class William J. VerMeulen. (William J. VerMeulen)

that could have proved deadly to all concerned. After dark, at approximately 1830, Major Meyer began leading his emergency strike flight out to the runway for take-off.

After receiving clearance from the tower and instructions to taxi to the middle of the runway, five of the seven Corsairs made their way to the center of the strip as there were no lights on the first half of the field. At the end of the unlit portion of the runway, 1st Lieutenant Richard A. Polen, in aircraft number 6, began his take-off roll. He quickly got to the center section of the runway where a cluster of VMF-121 FG's were sitting.

His plane struck 1st Lieutenant Andrew M. Kelly's Corsair, crushing the FG's turtle back and canopy. He also struck 1st Lieutenant James V. Holcombe's FG, damaging its port wing. Someone called the tower to close the field and this was quickly accomplished. Andy Kelly's Corsair sat disabled on the runway and he got out and ran clear. Seconds later, 1st Lieutenant Virginius B. Perry started his take-off roll from the darkened end of the runway. His FG struck 2nd Lieutenant Robert H. Hall's Corsair in the cockpit and also damaged Hill's left wing. Perry's FG suffered a damaged right wing in the crash.

Just when all concerned thought the worst was over, and when all aircraft were clear of the runway, except for Kelly's Corsair, Major Robert G. Snowden taxied out and began his take-off roll. Needless to say, he struck Kelly's abandoned FG, demolishing both aircraft. Snowden was seriously injured but would fully recover. Lieutenant Polen was able to get airborne but could not maintain control over his aircraft at low speeds. He had to bail out over the water and was later rescued.

What a night for Major Meyer's flight. Six of seven planes out of commission and not one shot fired in anger. Thankfully, no one lost his life.

On 12 November, Major Bill Clay led a flight of twelve fighters on a bombing mission to Gagil-Tomil airstrip on Yap Island. They left Peleliu at 1215. After the bombing and strafing runs had been completed, all the Corsairs rendezvoused off the southern tip of Yap. 2nd Lieutenant Jack E. Deen noticed signs of an oil leak coming from Bob Gillis's aircraft and called him to let him know what he had observed. Gillis radioed back that he thought he could make it back to Peleliu. Bill Clay said he thought it better to fly to Ulithi, which was 175 miles shorter than the distance to Peleliu. That was the plan, at least. A PBY was contacted and if followed ten miles behind.

The oil leak coming from Gillis' Corsair steadily became worse. Gillis would be forced to make a water landing. At approximately 1432, the landing was made and the FG remained afloat for about a minute. They were about fifty miles from Ulithi.

Lieutenant Gillis got out of his fighter and spread his dye marker on the water. Major Clay, Lieutenant Deen and 2nd Lieutenant Lloyd P.

Findholt all saw Gillis apparently safe in the water and circled him until the PBY arrived about twelve minutes later. The pilot of the PBY saw Gillis wave on his initial pass and landed his seaplane a short distance away. After landing the PBY, the pilot and crew could not find Gillis but did see his canteen float by. The rest of Clay's flight continued circling the area until 1610. Since their gas was running low and the PBY was taking on water, they had to leave the area and fly on to Ulithi. They arrived there at 1635. The loss of George Gillis was felt by all in the squadron.

Barge sweeps continued to be the order of the day. Most of these missions were carried out using a four plane division and went on all day long with flight times averaging about two and a half hours in length.

During November, the squadron began to receive the Vought F4U-1D fighter. Up until that time they had been flying mostly Goodyear FG-1As. The F4U-1D had an improved canopy without the metal framing, giving the pilot a much more improved field of view from the cockpit.

Major Meyer took a flight out at 1140 on 18 November, to bomb both Gagil-Tomil and Yap airfields. Meyer's mission was a complete success. Both airstrips were rendered unserviceable and they destroyed eight Japanese aircraft on the ground. 2nd Lieutenant J. Allan Carmena's FG was hit in the engine by anti-aircraft fire and he had to make a forced landing in the sea. He was picked-up by a PBY Catalina within five minutes and was back on Peleliu by 1230.

VMF-121 lost another pilot when Major Bill Clay was hit on 21 November while on a strafing run against Japanese barges and small boats along the shore of Yap Island. His Corsair exploded on impact.

An old friend, Phil Leeds, came back to the squadron as a guest pilot on 23 November. He stayed long enough to test hop one of the squadron's aircraft.

From time to time, VMF-121 pilots flew escort missions with other

VMF-121's Commanding Officer. Major Walter Meyer receives the Distinguished Flying Cross (DFC) from Marine General Christian F. Schilt during a ceremony on Peleliu, 2 May 1945. (Walter J. Meyer)

squadrons. Captain Hardy Hay led one such flight when they accompanied twelve TBF-1 Avengers of VMTB-232 to attack the airfield at Gagil-Tomil. The mission was a complete success.

Every so often, the pilots of VMF-121 would draw an assignment that would provide a little variety for them. On 8 December, Major Meyer led a flight of four aircraft to bomb the Point Bradford Lighthouse. They were accompanied by a four plane division led by Major Quintus "B" Nelson. Using skip bombing technics, Meyer placed his 1,000 pound bomb directly into the base of the target, destroying it completely.

By the end of 1944, the squadron had participated in almost daily sweeps against the Japanese barges found around the Palau Islands. The Christmas holiday proved a welcome relief from that dangerous routine.

The new year was only eleven days old when the squadron lost another fine pilot. Major Nelson and Lieutenant Hill each led a division against enemy targets on Urukthapel Island north of Peleliu. One revetted gun position was blown apart and the top of an adjacent lighthouse was blown over. Lieutenant Hill's flight flew against another coastal gun position on Babelthuap Island, the northernmost island in the Palau chain. This gun position was located near the Arumaten Point lighthouse. Bob Hill's men lined up to make their bomb run. One by one the attack was carried to the target. One of the Corsairs, flown by Lieutenant Perry, was seen to go down on land near the lighthouse. His plane burst into flames upon impact and Perry was considered killed. "Bobbie", as he was called, was a Mojave plank owner (a plank owner is an original member of the unit).

The story of Bobbie Perry has a chilling footnote. Years after the war, a group of Marines touring the Palau Islands came back with a tale as sung by the native tribes because they didn't or couldn't tell the story in words. They sung of a "baby face" Marine Lieutenant (or pilot) who was shot down and captured by the Japanese. In their singing story they related that the Japanese soldiers lead this pilot through the various tribes and said this was their enemy. The Japanese then led him back to their camp and beheaded him. Squadron members from the Peleliu time period feel this was Lieutenant Perry.

An attempt was made during the early morning hours of 18 January to land Japanese troops on Peleliu's Purple and White beaches. About fifty-four enemy soldiers came ashore; half to one beach, half to the other. Their landing barges had become stranded on a coral reef and they had to wade in. They managed to make it to a bushy area near the airfield. Marine guards were placed around the planes and an intense search was made throughout the day to find the Japanese troops. Eventually more than half of the landing party was found and killed. Upon questioning some of the prisoners, they revealed that the "invasion" force had came from the vicinity of Arakabesan Island where the Japanese had a submarine and seaplane base.

On the island of Koror, located just off the southern coast Babelthuap Island, the Japanese had established numerous gun positions concentrated on a high point on the island that became known as "Battery Hill."

On 4 March 1945, VMF-121 was given the job of taking this gun position out of action. It was to be a combined strike with other Marine squadrons being assigned similar duty against Japanese positions on Malakal and Arakabesan Islands. VMF-114 and VMF-122 were to carry out that part of the forty-eight aircraft strike force.

The F4Us and FGs of VMF-121 each carried one 325 pound depth charge on the first flight. The results of this first attack were very good and no one was lost. On the second run against "Battery Hill", the anti-aircraft fire was intense and accurate. Fortunately, the planes of 121 made it through OK.

On the third strike, the squadron's luck ran out. On this strike each plane carried one 1,000 pound General Purpose bomb. By now the anti-aircraft fire had really gotten heavy.

1st Lieutenant Walter F. Brown, leader of the second division on this flight, had just gotten into his dive on the target when his plane was hit under its cockpit by what was probably a 40MM round. The projectile

Former VMF-121 pilot, Major R. Bruce Porter, awards the Purple Heart Medal to Master Technical Sergeant John Rohrbach, also a former member of VMF-121 on 22 July 1945, Chimu, Okinawa. In the background is Captain Wallace E. Sigler, Executive Officer of VMF(N)-542. which was under the command of Major Porter. (John Rohrbach)

exploded at his feet. Brown's Corsair was now on fire and soon he was forced to bail out. Brown got half-way out of the cockpit and his left leg got caught. His leg had been hit by fragments from the exploding shell. His F4U, now flying at about 300 mph, was in its plunge toward the sea. Brown could not free himself and the wind of the slip-stream kept banging him repeatedly into the side of the aircraft. Finally, he was able to pull himself free and pull on his parachute ring. He was now hurtling through the air at a terrific speed. When his 'chute deployed, his knees were thrown up against his chin and one knee was dislocated.

Brown then looked down and saw some of his squadron mates pulling out of their dives. He also became aware that he was falling toward land and he did all he could to swing himself out toward the sea. The wind seemed to be against him and he didn't seem to be making any progress. As he got lower he reached for his sidearm but it was not there. Just then he noticed water below him. He then forgot about the Japanese and prepared for a water landing.

Brown landed in the water only about 100 yards from shore and close to a Japanese pier. His legs were all but useless but tried to swim just using his hands.

Patrol Squadron 23 (VP-23) PPC (Patrol Plane Commander) Lieutenant Commander Fred H. Mamer and his crew had been assigned "Dumbo" duty covering the third strike on Koror Island. Over his radio he heard that a fighter pilot had bailed out over the target. Just then he saw Brown's 'chute open and watched as he floated down to the water just off shore in the center of the harbor. Just then someone from VMF-121 called to him and asked if he had seen the pilot bail out. Mamer answered in the affirmative. Then the flight leader in the VMF-121 group told Mamer that the squadron would form a Lufberry Circle over his PBY and cover him with strafing during the rescue.

By now Mamer was seriously concerned about the chances of getting in to rescue Brown and getting away safely. After being assured by the 121 leader that they could pull it off, Mamer elected to give it a try. As they were going in, a burst of white phosphorus exploded just over Brown's position in the water. The concussions rocked the side of the PBY-5A. Despite misgivings about whether or not to risk the lives of the nine men in his crew for the life of one in the water, Mamer pressed on, determined to make the rescue.

Anti-aircraft fire was all around the Catalina as it descended toward Brown in the harbor. Mamer called to VMF-121 to get the guns on Arakabesan. VMF-121 complied. Just then another burst of fire exploded underneath the PBY and Mamer was sure they had been holed. A quick check proved the old flying boat was OK. Mamer started his second approach. The fighters gave him all the cover possible and it worked. He was able to land about 50 yards from Brown and started

HOME SWEET HOLLYWOOD... VMF-121's George Burianic (center) and friends, enjoy the nightlife at a Hollywood, California nightclub. By this time, Peleliu was history and getting home was the top priority. (George Burianic)

taxiing towards him.

Brown was just west of his dye marker, on his back and "splashing as hard as he could." One of the PBY crewmen threw him a line with a life ring attached. Brown caught the line but was then confronted with another problem. The PBY began weathercocking (swinging around into the fifteen/twenty knot wind). Mamer could not use the sea anchor as that might entangle Brown and pull him under water. The weathercocking effect of the wind pulled the tail of the PBY across Brown so that he was now on the starboard side with the line to him going under the hull. Brown had to let the line go. During all of this, shells were coming in from "Battery Hill" and Arakabesan, barely missing the rescue party.

Mamer decided to make another run on Brown and again the same thing happened. This time Mamer decided to go aft and see what he could do about the situation. It was now getting extremely dangerous and it had to be now or leave Brown behind. Shells were hitting all around, some so close that Mamer thought for a minute that they had been hit.

It was decided to forget the line. They would try to grab him and bring him into the side blister. As the PBY passed over Brown, he had the presence of mind to duck down to avoid the propeller and when he came up he was in a good position for the "hands on" rescue. As soon as they had Brown aboard the PBY, Second Pilot Ensign Philip E. Russell pushed the throttle forward and the PBY started its take-off run.

Once onboard and safely in the air, Brown's wounds were attended by Lt(jg) Roy M. Kash, a flight surgeon. The whole episode took less than one hour after Brown bailed out of his fighter.

The Pacific war kept moving along all around VMF-121. The Philippines campaign opened up with the landings on the east coast of Leyte on 20 October 1944. The first Marine Corps squadron to operate from Leyte came from Peleliu, VMF(N)-541 with their twelve F6F-5Ns. They came into Tacloban on 3 December 1944. Many Marine aviation units fought in the campaign and sitting on Peleliu, VMF-121 wondered if they too would be sent over to the Philippines.

Manila fell to the Americans on 3 March 1945. The city was devastated. Over three quarters of the once beautiful "Pearl of the Orient" was left in ruins. There was still months of fighting left in the Japanese occupiers, but the end was in sight and General Douglas MacArthur had made his "I shall return" pledge a reality. He came ashore on Corregidor on 2 March 1945. On 2 March VMF-121 flew their usual barge sweeps.

The massive assault on Iwo Jima took place on 19 February 1945. Marine squadrons were now operating from aircraft carriers. VMFs-112 and 123 flew from the USS BENNINGTON (CV-20), VMFs -221 and 451 were on the USS BUNKER HILL (CV-17) VMFs-124 and 213

were based on the USS ESSEX (CV-9) and VMFs-216 and 217 were operating from USS WASP (CV-18). All were flying the F4U-1D Corsair.

The Iwo Jima battle lasted until 14 March 1945. Some fanatic Japanese held out until 21 March, but were quickly disposed of. The island provided yet another airfield that much closer to Japan.

Easter Sunday, 1 April 1945, saw the beginning of the last battle of the Second World War. Again the top prize was the island's two airfields, Yontan and Kadena. Marine aviation played a large role in this last battle. Marine and Navy pilots were kept busy trying to down the rain of Kamikaze suicide pilots that were thrown into the battle. Marine squadrons accounted for 506 Japanese aircraft shot down during the Okinawa fight.

On all previous combat tours VMF-121 had always been tested in air-to-air combat. On their fourth and final tour, the squadron shot down only one enemy aircraft. This was due to the almost total lack of enemy air activity in the Palau Islands area. The enemy aircraft were just not there for VMF-121 pilots to engage. The only chance for combat happened over Ulithi Atoll on 28 April 1945.

Six VMF-121 pilots were assigned to Ulithi to assist in combat air patrol over the big Navy base. Major Meyer and his pilots knew that the Japanese were overflying Ulithi everyday with one of their reconnaissance aircraft. It would come over at 32,000 feet and Major Meyer was determined to get it. Two of the units F4Us were stripped of all their armor and two of the aircraft's six guns were removed to enable the Corsairs to reach the altitude the Japanese operated at. Four Army P-51s from Guam were also on hand at Ulithi during this time period. On the day of the scramble, 121's two F4Us took off, followed by two of the P-51s. Bob Hill and 1st Lieutenant George C. Huntington were flying the Corsairs. The two pilots located the Japanese Myrt and closed in for the kill. The Japanese aircraft was quickly shot down and each pilot was credited with half a kill, the last scored by pilots from VMF-121.

On 2 May, during a small ceremony, Major Meyers received the Distinguished Flying Cross (DFC) for his heroism and extraordinary achievement while participating in aerial flight in the Western Carolines from 30 October 1944 to 28 February 1945.

New pilots started trickling into the squadron during the Spring of 1945. Bill Lundin came in on 8 May. Lundin had flown with 121 on the squadron's second tour on Guadalcanal.

The squadron continued to send small groups of pilots to Ultihi on a daily basis throughout May.

The squadron acquired a new Commanding Officer on 26 May when

Technical Sergeant Frank J. Mayer (left) his brother Sergeant John J. Mayer, USA and a friend, at their Santa Ana, California, home in 1945. (Frank J. Mayer)

Major Claude H. Welch relieved Major Meyer. Bill Lundin was also named squadron Executive Officer. Walter Meyer had served as commander of VMF-121 longer than any other commanding officer, eighteen months.

The FG-1A Corsair was slowly being deleted from VMF-121's inventory. On 31 May, the squadron transferred seven FG-1s out of the unit and brought in seven F4U-1Ds from VMF-114.

Major Welch's tenure lasted until 12 June. The next day, Major Robert Tucker took over as commander. Bill Lundin stayed on as XO.

By this time, June of 1945, pilots were rotating stateside and new pilots were coming aboard. Thirteen came in on 9 June with ten more arriving three days later.

On 12 June, thirty pilots from VMF-121 were awarded the Air Medal and two Gold Stars in lieu of the second and third Air Medals for fifteen fighter-bomber missions in the Western Carolines area. George Huntington and Bob Hill received a fourth star for their Air Medals for their part in downing that Japanese plane over Ulithi.

Most VMF-121 pilots who had started the fourth tour were now on their way stateside by 21 June. They were very enthusiastic to say the least.

The new skipper, Major Tucker, got his feet wet during a strafing mission over the southeastern tip of Babelthuap Island. On 24 June, he made his run over the target area where his F4U was hit hard by anti-aircraft fire. The damage was such that Tucker had to make a forced landing in the water. Fortunately, he was able to pick an area where a Navy LCI (Landing Craft Infantry) boat was on station. He was picked up almost immediately.

VMF-121's Sergeant Tony Betchik at home in Cleveland, Ohio during 1945. (Tony Betchik)

PEACE! IT'S WONDERFUL...Home at last and ready to get on with their lives, many of VMF-121's personnel started that phase of their lives with a wedding like Technical Sergeant Francis J. Mayer and his bride, at the start of their life together on 8 July 1945. (Frank J. Mayer)

More pilots were shipped out on 26 June. Bill Lundin continued to lead strikes against the Japanese during the remainder of the month.

As of 30 June 1945, the squadron had only one ace on its roster, 1st Lieutenant William P. Brown with seven victories. Bill Lundin was next with 4.5 followed by 1st Lieutenant Norman Turley with four.

As the war progressed, the squadron became a revolving door for pilots coming in and pilots shipping out.

On 31 July, the squadron turned over twenty-one of their Corsairs, two F4U-1Ds, eleven FG-1As and eight FG-1Ds to VMF-122. The next day VMF-121 transferred forty-nine pilots to VMF-122 including Major Lundin. This made the squadron almost non-existent.

On 9 August 1945, 1st Lieutenant Richard M. Loughery, a squadron member since Mojave days, took command. Loughery was now responsible for taking the squadron's remaining members back to the states. He and six other veterans boarded the SS LOOKOUT on 10 August. They arrived at San Francisco, California on 6 September 1945. Three days later, at Miramar, Loughery transferred the following men to the base Personnel Group:

Master Technical Sergeant Oscar L. Golden, Jr. (Squadron Sergeant Major)

Master Technical Sergeant Chester H. Wright

Technical Sergeant Richard D. Kern

Staff Sergeant Ernest L. Kinney

Sergeant Richard T. Hayden

Sergeant Robert M. Ludwig

With that completed, Lieutenant Loughery signed off the final order and VMF-121 was decommissioned on 9 September 1945, authorized by Marine Corps Dispatch #051702.

Commanding Officers of VMF-121 During World War II

Many available sources were consulted during the compilation of this list. Most sources made comment that the dates shown may not be totally accurate. This is understandable owing to the fast pace at which wartime events often moved. Records sometimes had to take a backseat to whatever was going on at the time. Later, when time permitted, these things were recorded from memory. So even in the case of squadron CO's, exact dates may have suffered a little.

Taking all things into consideration, the author decided to use the VMF-121 War Diaries and Robert Sherrod's fine book "HISTORY OF MARINE CORPS AVIATION IN WORLD WAR II" as his source in the matter.

Major Samuel S. Jack, 24 June 1941 - 28 February 1942
Captain Leonard K. Davis, 1 March 1942 - 16 December 1942
Lieutenant William F. Wilson, 17 - 31 December 1942
Major Donald K. Yost, 1 January 1943 - 12 March 1943
Major Joseph N. Renner, 13 - 26 March 1943
Major Raymond L. Vroome, 27 March - 31 July 1943
Captain Robert E. Bruce, 1 - 23 August 1943
1st Lieutenant Henry O. DeFries, 24 August 1943 - 24 October 1943
Captain Quintus "B" Nelson, 25 October 1943 - 30 November 1943
Major Walter J. Meyer, 1 December 1943 - 25 May 1945
Major Claude H. Welch, 26 May 1945 - 12 June 1945
Major Robert Tucker,13 June 1945 - 31 July 1945
1st Lieutenant Richard M. Loughery, 1 August 1945 - 9 September 1945

Japanese Aircraft Destroyed

VMF-121 was officially credited by the Marine Corps with a total of 208 enemy aircraft shot down. Post war studies have revised this figure from 208 to 209. The 209 figure includes the 3.5 shot down by 2nd Lieutenant Thomas H. Mann, Jr. while he was on STAD to VMF-224 in late September and early October 1942. The revised figure also included the one victory scored by 2nd Lieutenant Floyd A. Lynch while he was on STAD to VMF-223 during early-October 1942.MEDAL OF HONOR RECIPIENTS - VMF-121

Captain Joseph J. Foss   Guadalcanal, 9 October 1942 - 26 January 1943

VMF-121 Aces

Many squadron pilots qualified as Ace during their tour with VMF-121 including: 2nd Lieutenant William "B" Freeman, 2nd Lieutenant Joseph L. Narr, Captain Joseph J. Foss, 2nd Lieutenant Roger A. Haberman, Major Leonard K. Davis, 2nd Lieutenant Gregory K. Loesch, 2nd Lieutenant Thomas H. Mann, 2nd Lieutenant William P. Marontate, 2nd Lieutenant Cecil J. Doyle, Major Donald K. Yost, 1st Lieutenant Elton Mueller, Captain Francis E. Pierce, Captain Kenneth M. Ford, Captain Perry L. Shuman, Captain Robert M. Baker

Many more VMF-121 pilots started on their path to becoming an Ace while with the squadron: Captain Joseph Hunter Reinburg, 1st Lieutenant Herbert H. Long, 2nd Lieutenant Frank H. Presley, 1st Lieutenant William M. Lundin, 1st Lieutenant Henry A. McCartney, Captain R. Bruce Porter

One VMF-121 pilot, 1st Lieutenant William P. Brown, was an Ace before he joined the squadron.

Honor Roll

VMF-121 Pilots Killed Or Missing In Action

2nd Lieutenant George A. Treptow (Flying of STAD with VMF-223)	10-2-42	Guadalcanal
2nd Lieutenant Paul S. Rutledge	10-14-42	Guadalcanal
MTSgt. Alexander Thomson, NAP	10-14-42	Guadalcanal
2nd Lieutenant Wiley H. Craft	10-17-42	Guadalcanal
2nd Lieutenant Floyd A. Lynch	10-18-42	Guadalcanal
2nd Lieutenant Edward P. Andrews	10-19-42	Guadalcanal
2nd Lieutenant Eugene A. Nuwer	10-20-42	Guadalcanal
Marine Gunner Henry B. Hamilton, NAP, flying on STAD from VMF-212)	10-21-42	Guadalcanal
TSgt. Emmet L. Anderson, NAP, flying on STAD from VM0-251)	10-21-42	Guadalcanal
2nd Lieutenant Cecil J. Doyle	11-7-42	Guadalcanal
2nd Lieutenant Roy M.A. Ruddell	11-11-42	Guadalcanal
2nd Lieutenant Joseph L. Narr	11-11-42	Guadalcanal
2nd Lieutenant Robert F. Simpson	11-11-42	Guadalcanal
MTSgt. Joseph J. Palko, NAP	11-11-42	Guadalcanal
2nd Lieutenant Koller C. Brandon	11-14-42	Guadalcanal
Lieutenant Colonel Harold F. Bauer (Flying on STAD from VMF-212)	11-14-42	Guadalcanal
1st Lieutennat Donald S. Meyers	12-3-42	Guadalcanal
Marine Gunner Benjamin B. Wisner, NAP	12-23-42	Guadalcanal
2nd Lieutenant Yovell L. Crum	1-2-43	Guadalcanal
2nd Lieutenant Robert L. Petersen	1-2-43	Guadalcanal
Captain Irwin W. Carter	1-4-43	Guadalcanal
1st Lieutenant Joseph E. Cannon	1-11-43	Guadalcanal
1st Lieutenant William P. Marontate	1-15-43	Guadalcanal
Captain E.M. Schmidt	6-12-43	Guadalcanal
1st Lieutenant William H. Snee	6-28-43	Banika
Captain Louis Gordon	6-30-43	Russell Islands
1st Lieutenant Caruth A. Barker, Jr.	7-2-43	Russell Islands
1st Lieutenant George O. Beal	10-31-43	Russell Islands
2nd Lieutenant Robert L. Gillis	11-12-44	Peleliu
Major William Clay	11-21-44	Peleliu
2nd Lieutenant Virginius B. Perry	01-11-45	Peleliu
2nd Lieutenant Thomas H. O'Boyle	03-13-45	Peleliu

Enlisted Personnel Killed In Action With VMF-121

Corporal Joseph S. Bruno	10-23-42	Guadalcanal
Sergeant Richard C. Milage	10-3-44	Peleliu
Private First Class Ernest B. Deaton	Date unkn.	Peleliu
Sergeant Truman L. Malicoat	Date unkn.	Peleliu